SO
WHAT'S
NEXT?

Tom Bathgate

CHRISTIAN FOCUS PUBLICATIONS
OM PUBLISHING

Bible quotations are from the New International Version, published by Hodder and Stoughton or The Bible in Today's English Version published by the Bible Societies

© 1992 Tom Bathgate

ISBN 1 871 676 843 (Christian Focus)
ISBN 1 85078 112 5 (OM)

Christian Focus Publications Ltd
Geanies House, Fearn, Ross-shire,
IV20 1TW, Scotland, Great Britain.

OM Publishing is an imprint of Send The Light
(Operation Mobilisation), PO Box 300,
Carlisle, Cumbria, CA3 0QS, England

Printed and bound in Great Britain
by Cox & Wyman Ltd, Reading

Cover design
by
Seoris N. McGillivray

Photograph
from
ZEFA Picture Library (UK) Ltd

CONTENTS

Dedicated
To Edgar
My late father-in-law
My friend, hero and encourager
Missed and loved more than ever.

FOREWORD

After years of replying to letters from confused and often 'desperate' young people, spending hours in counselling and communicating to many thousands of teenagers, I discovered that there was a genuine lack of good written material that I could recommend to them. I don't mean Smash Hits, 19, NME or even a 4-inch thick Bible commentary! . . . none of which are in short supply. What is needed are books that are culturally relevant, easy to read, honest, biblical and above all helpful.

When I was sent a copy of *So What's Next?* I became really excited as it has managed to capture all the above ingredients. As a book it not only will help those already in difficulties, but being so honest and 'normal' in facing the changes that take place in teenage years it will also prevent many succumbing to the heat of temptation and to the pressures from today's society.

I've known Tom for some time and respect him greatly, not just because he's a fellow Scot(!), but because he's one of God's 'marked out' men called for such a time as this. His passion for Jesus and compassion for others is evident to all who meet him and gives tremendous authority and credibility to the things he's written in this book.

God is looking for a new generation of disciples who will be recklessly obedient to him. *So What's Next?* will help you understand more about yourself, more about the pressures you experience and give you a pathway that will help you become part of this new generation.

Ray Goudie
Director
New Generation Ministries

INTRODUCTION

I was surprised to discover recently that the word 'adolescence' is actually a twentieth century word. That doesn't mean that adolescents have been invented in this century, but rather that the term is relatively new. It simply means 'the period of growth to maturity', and that's what this book is about. It's recognising first of all that you are a person in process! You have not arrived! You are on the way.

That means that you are constantly involved in change. Change involves the unknown, the new, which always produces some degree of pressure. Part 2 will look at the fact that you are a person under all sorts of pressure. It's pretty obvious that if you are moving from something to something, and you are at a transitional stage of your life, then the something that you are moving towards is full of great potential. And that's what part 3 deals with: the fact that you are a person with great potential. The person you become will, without doubt, be shaped by the people you know, the decisions you make, the priorities and goals you set, the prayers you pray and the games you play.

These are major ingredients of the process you are in, the pressure you face and the reaching of your full potential.

A few years ago at an international youth camp in Northern Ireland I saw a brilliant poster on a classroom wall which read, 'Make a book happy - read it!'

Happy reading.

Tom Bathgate

People
In
Process

Part
1

Jesus
The
Adolescent

Chapter 1

As I've been writing this book, my wife has given birth to our third child. He's a little boy and he's a real cracker! I wish you could see and touch him. He's bald, soft, tender, tiny and cuddly. He is an expert at filling his nappy but he has won all our hearts. There's a loving competition going on between our other two, Timothy and Joanna, to see who can touch him first, hold him the longest and kiss him the most. Stuart just laps it all up, unless his big brother and sister turn him into a lollipop and lick him so much that he can't take any more and then he cries!

It dawned on me one day that Jesus was once a baby and that he did not suddenly appear as a thirty year old man. He actually grew up! Just as Stuart came into the world as a baby, so did Jesus. What a shock it would have been for us if my wife Angela had given birth to a thirty year old man - what a thought!

Then I found in Luke's Gospel that 'Jesus grew in wisdom and stature, and in favour with God and man' (Luke 2:52 N.I.V.).

It was even more enlightening to discover that the word for 'grow' used by Luke means 'to make one's way forward by pushing aside obstacles'. Initially it was used to describe a ship sailing to its destination through the hazards of the high seas or an army hacking its way through a forest or crossing a river in spate.

Just imagine Jesus hacking his way through adolescence! Jesus knows what it's like to go through that tough and temporary stage between childhood and adulthood known as adolescence.

He, like us, had to come to terms with the fact that we are all people in process. None of us have arrived. We are all 'on the way' from one stage of our lives to the next. The reason? We were born in order to grow!

In my late teens I started visiting some sick children in hospital. At the end of one particular visit, just as I was leaving, I passed a lady who was really upset.

I stopped to ask if I could help. She said that it was impossible to help her. I asked her why? She then proceeded to tell me the tragic and painful story of her little boy who was just over two years old. The major problem was that he had stopped growing and there was nothing that could be done.

As I travelled home I realised something for the first time. Growing up may be tough and complicated, but it's not as painful as not growing at all.

A few months ago I witnessed a parent-child dedication taking place. I looked at the young mum, who with her husband had come to dedicate themselves and their child to the Lord. As I looked at her I thought, 'You have certainly made your way forward by pushing aside huge obstacles.' Obstacles like being taken away from her parents as a young teenager, experiencing the same kind of abuse from her foster dad as she had from her own, choosing to go it alone as she pursued her career, living through the stormy relationship with her step-dad, existing in her teenage years with deep rejection.

But how she has grown. She has hacked her way through the forest of obstacles that I've just mentioned and grown into a buoyant, committed wife and mum. She had discovered that she was a person in process, a person born to grow and that the future is not always as difficult and dark as the past.

Adolescence, or as I said in the introduction 'the period of growth to maturity' is not primarily a problem, it's a process, and we all have to go through it. It's normal, it's OK, it's acceptable and you can't avoid it! Don't believe the TV adverts - those zitless coca-cola kids are a myth!

Luke, who wrote about the fact that Jesus grew, was actually a Doctor. He was obviously very well educated and was also interested in things that were apparently not of interest to Matthew, Mark or John. As far as I can discover the Jews divided a child's growth into eight different stages from birth through to adulthood. Doctor Luke seems to reduce those stages to two. He describes Jesus' growth in this way:

<> "... the child grew and became strong; He was filled with wisdom and the grace of God was upon him" (Luke 2:40 N.I.V.).

<> "... Jesus grew in wisdom and stature, and in favour with God and men" (Luke 2:52 N.I.V.).

In this description of Jesus at the start of his teens, Doctor Luke shows us that even the Lord Jesus moved through different stages of his development.

In the rest of Part 1 we want to explore the different stages that Luke highlights. Before we do that, here is a prayer to pray and a question to answer.

Prayer

Thank you, Lord Jesus, that you understand the process that I'm going through at this stage of my life.

It's good to know that even at this point in my life I can follow you because you have been through adolescence.

In your Name,
Amen

Question

What three words would you choose to describe the particular part of the process that you are going through right now?

1.

2.

3.

Hellish
or
Heavenly Wisdom

Chapter 2

Experts tell me that adolescence is often divided into three periods. Here they are:

< > Early adolescence - which begins around the age of ten or eleven.

< > Middle adolescence - which involves those years from about age fifteen to eighteen.

< > Late adolescence - which starts approximately at age eighteen and extends into the twenties.

These experts tell me that the first period begins with an eruption of biological changes which can produce feelings of anxiety, bewilderment and delight. Both sexes have a 'spurt of growth' which produces a change in body proportions. Girls expand in the hips and develop breasts, boys go wider in the shoulders and develop thicker muscles. Girls begin their menstrual cycle, boys have an enlargement of sexual organs, the growth of pubic hair, a lowering of their voice and both have an increase in the size of their skin pores which leads to you know what!

I'm also told that over the past one hundred years there has been a steady lowering of the age at which girls begin their menstrual cycle and boys first emit semen. This means that adolescence is getting earlier and earlier in life. With all of this comes the influence and pressure of peers and a new spirit of independence from parents.

Middle adolescence has fewer physical changes but the struggle to adapt and cope as a person living with an adult body is not easy. Sexual urges remain intense and difficult to control especially when society no longer considers self-control to be a high priority. (Within recent years there has been a remarkable increase in the number of births to teenagers, most of whom are unmarried.) The peers who were important during the first period take an even greater significance during this one.

It's during middle adolescence that teenagers attempt to break away from the influence, values and regulations of parents. They often do not want to go with their parents to church, on holiday or on those horrendous shopping trips. Communication at home can become minimal, daydreaming and hours on the telephone talking with friends is the status-quo. There is an incredible desire to be accepted and to be wearing the right clothes, using the trendy words and listening to the latest music. Building relationships with the opposite sex becomes a high priority and painful moments can be experienced when break-ups occur.

It's during this period that sex, drugs, cars and motorbikes move up the agenda. The sexual openness in our society and the easy access to condoms and privacy make sexual intercourse a common experience. The use of drugs, including alcohol invades this stage of the process, especially for those who are looking for a weird experience or trying to run away from pressure or boredom or seeking acceptance from their drinking and drug-using friends. Joyriding or charging about on motorbikes in weird ways and at odd times can become a way of expressing anger, coping with boredom or becoming acceptable to the opposite sex.

I remember early one morning, in my late teens going to collect the newspapers that I was responsible for delivering. I was shattered by what I saw and read on the front page of a national newspaper. A friend of mine, who had just turned twenty, and was part of a Christian youth group that I belonged to, was found dying from a drugs' overdose on the back seat of a car. He was a Christian and someone I looked up to, but nevertheless he had fallen prey to the lure of the drug experience.

As teenagers move into late adolescence this interest in drugs, vehicles and sex continues. During this period the young person has to face the task of moving into adult society, picking up adult responsibilities and beginning to 'go solo' as well as form a distinct life style. Planning for the future, developing a career, choosing a partner absorbs an incredible amount of time and energy. The three 'mega' questions during this period are: Who am I? How do I relate to others? and What should I believe? The attempt to answer these questions can produce confusion, emptiness, stress but also fulfilment.

Who would choose to go through this period of growth to maturity? It's no wonder that the word used to describe Jesus growing was the one which described a ship sailing to its destination through the hazards of the high seas or an army hacking its way through a forest or crossing a river in spate! You might almost think that these three periods of life are to be avoided like the plague! Before you think too long on that, let me remind you what the writer of Ecclesiastes says to young men and women:

> "... it's wonderful to be young! Enjoy every minute of it! Do all you want to; take in everything, but realise that you must account to God for everything you do. So banish grief and pain, but remember that youth, with a whole life before it, can make serious mistakes" (Eccles. 11:9,10 Living Bible).

What is also brilliant is that Jesus went through adolescence. We know from Doctor Luke that Jesus grew but we also know from what he tells us the different areas in which he grew. In the rest of this chapter I want to look at the fact that Jesus grew in wisdom.

Jesus grew in Wisdom

I suppose that in order to know what Luke means we need to discover what wisdom is.

Proverbs 1:7 informs us that the beginning of wisdom is the fear of the Lord. So to say that Jesus grew in wisdom is simply another way of saying that he lived in the fear of God. The mention of the 'fear of God' is almost strange and unwanted to our modern ears. That's how I responded when I heard of it for the first time.

One day, however, an old Christian man told me this little story which helped me to understand a little of what the fear of God is. Two small boys, he told me, were looking into a shop window. It was crammed full with lots of things that they didn't have, couldn't afford and desperately wanted. Nobody was about and the shop was closed for the night. They began to talk about smashing the window and stealing what they wanted. Eventually one boy said, 'If I do this, my dad will kill me.' At that point the other answered, 'If I do it, it will kill my dad.'

My old Christian friend then said, 'That's what it is to fear the Lord; it is to love our heavenly Father so much that we would be ashamed to do anything that would displease or hurt him. It's to love him so much that we are happiest when we are pleasing him.' So wisdom is recognising who God is, seeing things from his point of view and choos-

21

ing your attitudes and making your decisions in order to please him.

I have a friend who spends most of his time teaching the Bible in schools. He was telling me that in senior school, young people get pumped full of information and often they don't know what to do with it. They also carry such a workload that there isn't a lot of time to stop, pause and evaluate how to apply the information. As I was thinking what that must be like I remembered something James said.

Two kinds of wisdom

He said that there are two kinds of wisdom in this world and they come from different sources. On the one hand there is a wisdom that 'does not come down from heaven but is earthly, unspiritual and of the devil'; on the other, there is a wisdom that 'comes from heaven' (James 3:13,17). So as far as James is concerned our wisdom is either *hellish* or *heavenly*; it's either from God or the devil. That kind of information is pretty serious stuff!

How does this work out in practice? Take for instance the whole business of authority. When you were a little child growing up, you didn't know that was what it was called, but you knew how it felt. Your mum and dad seemed to be full of it and it always meant that you had to do what they said - or else! Then comes school and you learned some more about authority. How it should and shouldn't be. You learned all kinds of things about the authority of governments, armies, politicians and head-teachers! But then, somebody needs to say to you, 'By the way, all this information about authority is very important, because you have to decide how to handle authority.' At that point, you will then begin to draw on heavenly or hellish wisdom or a bit of both!

You have to look at your attitude towards your parents or your teacher or your coach and discover what is your present response or reaction to authority. Remember, your attitude will be seen in your actions towards those particular people.

Hellish wisdom is often seen in decisions that are made out of envy, self-interest and selfish ambition. Heavenly wisdom will be found by asking the question, 'What's God's view of this and how does he want me to respond?' Heavenly wisdom will then choose to please God no matter the cost or the consequence.

That's how Jesus lived, even as a teenager. He chose to please his heavenly Father no matter the cost or the consequence. It seems to me that the choices he made as a teenager to please his heavenly Father were part of the process of 'learning obedience' which prepared him to choose the cross.

It may seem foolish to many people, but the

greatest display of Heavenly wisdom was when Jesus said, 'Not my will but your will be done.' It was very costly for Jesus to die, but because he had hacked his way through the forest of adolescence in the 'fear of God', he was able in his adult life to make that supreme choice to die our death, endure our pain and pay the price for our sin. The choices you make now will profoundly influence the choices you make as an adult. Go for heavenly wisdom every time - Jesus did!

Prayer

Thank you, Lord Jesus for making your choices and living your life on the basis of heavenly and not hellish wisdom.

Help me to identify each kind as I live in society.

Show me how to build my relationships, spend my time, respond to authority and enjoy being young on the basis of heavenly wisdom.

In your name,
Amen

Questions

According to these verses in God's Word, what does 'fearing God' produce?

1. Psalm 112:1,7; The person who fears the Lord will have no fear ____ _____.

2. Exodus 20:20; Fearing God will keep you from _____.

3. Exodus 1:15-21; Because the Hebrew midwives feared God they would not kill the

_____ _____.

Did Jesus have 'dropsy'?

Chapter 3

Last night while we were having our evening meal, Sue, my sister-in-law dropped a plate. I said in fun, 'Feel free to drop as many as you like.' As we were laughing her mum said, 'She suffers from "dropsy" you know, ever since she was a teenager.' That comment then took us down memory lane and produced loads of laughter.

Sue told us of one incident which resulted in her dad giving her his one and only talk on the 'birds and the bees'.

Having dropped something in the kitchen she ran as fast as she could to her bedroom crying and screaming. She knew that if she had remained

down-stairs her mum would have disciplined her but if she ran to her room then it would be her dad who would come and assume the role of peace-maker!

In the process of making peace he attempted to explain why she was dropping things so regularly. This is how it went. The problem was the stage of growing up that she was at: her arms and legs had grown so fast and so much that her brain couldn't keep up with them! Therefore, the messages being sent from her brain to her arms couldn't be carried out properly, which meant that her co-ordination was not operating as it should. So she dropped things! She discovered that adolescence, this weird and wonderful period of growth to maturity, can bring in its wake 'dropsy', which according to her dad was because her brain was out of touch with the growth rate of her arms and legs. What a laugh we had together over that explanation!

I wonder if the Lord went through similar experiences during his adolescence.

Jesus grew in stature

Doctor Luke not only tells us that Jesus grew, and that he grew in wisdom, but also that he grew in stature. So perhaps he did go through 'dropsy' after all. These growing up years have their own peculiar and particular problems. Several factors can create these problems. For example:

< > Physical Changes can create spurts in growth, skin problems, excess fat, periodic decrease in energy, changes in body proportions, development of body hair, altering of voice pitch. When it is unbelievably important to look right and attractive, these changes can cause embarrassment and frustration, especially if the changes are slow in coming.

< > Sexual Changes are obviously expected but most young people get anxious over the physical changes without and the erotic impulses within. Masturbation, fantasising and adolescent intercourse can all produce guilt. Experiencing a crush on people of the same sex can lead to fears of homosexuality.

< > Relationship Changes occur with parents, peers and others in society. It is vital to be liked and accepted by peers, especially the opposite sex. Someone once said that it's when the inner and outer worlds seem to be changing that the young person begins to challenge adult authority.

< > Values change in a powerful way. Before adolescence young people accept the standards, guidelines and beliefs of their parents without much challenge or questioning. During

adolescence a personal set of values and beliefs begin to be formed. It's at this point that often doubt is expressed, involvement in Christian activities decreases, and turning to some other faith can be common. This produces a lot of stress for parents, especially when they realise that their children are being informed and influenced by equally confused and struggling peers.

< > Identity changes: When I lived and worked in Northern Ireland I saw the James Dobson film on the family. I don't remember a great deal of what I watched, however, I do remember him saying something about three things that teenagers feel they need in order to feel good about themselves: physical attractiveness, academic ability and money. Very rarely do the majority experience all three. As a result, feelings of incompetence, self-condemnation and failure can lead to an 'identity crisis'. During that period questions like, *What am I worth?* or *Where do I fit?* or *Who do I follow?* or *What is the purpose of my life?* are high on the agenda.

Without doubt, 'growing in stature' brings particular and peculiar problems, and these are all part of the process that we go through at this particular point in our lives.

A lovely little family that I know have just completed a two year process of treatment for their little girl who suffers from Leukaemia. One of the most important factors that helped them cope and continue was meeting other families who were experiencing similar trauma and passing through the same process. I've heard the parents say a number of times how good it was to share, sympathise and learn from others who knew exactly what it was like to be in their situation. Well, if you are 'growing in stature', the good news is that the Lord Jesus knows exactly what it's like to be in your situation.

That's what Graham Kendrick wrote about in his song:

> He walked where I walk
> He stood where I stand
> He felt what I feel,
> He understands,
> He knows my frailty
> Shared my humanity
> Tempted in ev'ry way
> Yet without sin.
>
> God with us, so close to us
> God with us, Immanuel.

Read them again, this time out loud! Go on! Go for it! If you know the tune, sing them! Go on! Go for it! He understands. He really does. He understands me!

On the 31st March 1968, at thirteen years of age, I asked the Lord Jesus to forgive my sins and to come and live in my life. He did that by giving me the gift of the Holy Spirit. God's Spirit makes Jesus real in us and sets about the huge task of making us like Jesus in our attitudes, reactions, motives and actions. As I began to seek to know the Lord and please him, the Holy Spirit began to make me increasingly conscious of Christ's presence with and within me. Through the work of God's Spirit I realised that the Lord himself was not only with me but was leading me through the areas of change that I mentioned earlier in the chapter. The knowledge that he understood, that he was always with me, that he was willing to lead and help me, enabled me to obey and trust him even though it was really difficult at times.

I have a number of favourite books. Among them are the *Chronicles of Narnia* by C. S. Lewis. In *The Horse and His Boy* there is a very special part of the story for me. Shasta, that's the boy, is going through a pretty tough adventure. He's very tired, lonely, a bit afraid and beginning to feel sorry for himself. As he is sitting on the Horse, crying in the dark as it travels at walking pace, suddenly he's aware that someone was walking beside him. He had no idea who or what it was or how long it had been there. Eventually he overcomes his shock and fear, asks who the person is and discovers something very special.

In the course of his adventure, Shasta had gone through some dangerous experiences and faced some tough problems. On a number of occasions a lion or lions had intervened and from his point of view, had either helped or hurt him. As he told this person in the pitch dark about his 'sorrows' he, to Shasta's amazement replied, 'I was the lion who forced you to join with Aravis. I was the cat who comforted you among the houses of the dead. I was the lion who drove the jackals from you while you slept. I was the lion who gave the horses the new strength of fear for the last mile so that you should reach King Lune in time. And I was the lion you do not remember who pushed the boat in which you lay, a child near death, so that it came to shore where a man sat, wakeful at midnight, to receive you.'

The next day Shasta had to travel, on his return journey by the same route. As he was travelling along the hillside path, it became narrower all the time and the drop to his right became steeper. While he was travelling along the edge of what he could now see was a precipice, he realised, and shuddered in the process, that he had been there the night before without realising it. But he had been quite safe! The lion had kept to his left.

Aslan had walked between him and the edge all the time!

That's what Jesus does with and for us when we are living in a relationship with him of faith and obedience. Many centuries ago he told his disciples that he would never leave, fail, forget or neglect his own. He will be with us at every stage of the process. Whoever we are, wherever we are, whatever the 'precipice' and however 'dark' it might be around us as we travel through the 'changes' he will never let us down.

Centuries before that he had proved his unfailing Presence to a teenager called Joseph. As Joseph goes through the process of moving out of middle into late adolescence he is rejected by his brothers, sold as a slave and ends up in another country and culture. Did the Lord forsake and forget him? No way! As you read the story in the book of Genesis, one phrase gets repeated on a number of occasions. Moses, the writer, does that so the reader will not miss the central truth of the story which is: 'The Lord was with him'. And not only was the Lord's presence a reality in his adolescence but it was because the Lord was there that he matured through the process, overcame the pressures and achieved his God-given potential.

'Growing in stature' can have its fun moments as I discovered with my sister-in-law and her dropsy. It definitely is a time of change that can produce its own set of problems. The Lord Jesus, however, knows exactly what it's like and he will not drop you! What was true for Joseph can be true for us.

Prayer

I'm so glad, Lord that you have been with teenagers like Joseph. It helps me know that I can experience your Presence too.

I'm also glad that you know what it's like to 'grow in stature'. It means that you feel what I feel; therefore you understand.

I trust in your unfailing Presence,
Amen.

Question

As far as these verses are concerned, what did Jesus promise his followers?

1. Matthew 18:20; That he would be _____

_____ _____

2. John 14:21; Those whose love for him is demonstrated by their obedience to him will discover Jesus _____ _____ to them.

Quality
Relationships

Chapter 4

It had been a very special evening for me. For weeks I had worked towards asking her to come out with me. Eventually courage came and when she agreed to going out for a meal, I was 'over the moon'.

We were making our way back to Edinburgh bus station and I was silently thinking, while my heart was pounding so hard that I was convinced passers-by were hearing it. 'I must hold her hand!' So I decided that after a count of three I would grab her hand. The count started 1...2...3...4... 5...6... and went to about forty! 'Come on Bathgate,' I said, 'are you a man or a mouse?'

I began the count once more and failed to 'seize the day', no 'seize the hand!' Finally I gave up counting, heard myself say 'go for it', so I did and managed to grab her leather shoulder bag that was hanging just below waist level. Being a Scotsman, I concluded that she probably thought I was going for her money. In order to correct that untrue view of a male Scot and to achieve my objective of 'seizing her hand', I nipped round to her other side, apologising about the shoulder bag incident and seized her right hand with my left hand. Wow! I made it! Inside I'm shouting, 'I'm in a relationship!' Did I feel good or did I feel good?

It was a relationship that was enjoyable but temporary.

Have you ever thought about the Lord's first recorded statement about his creature, Man? It tells us a lot about God's purpose for people.

'It's not good for the man to be alone' (Genesis 2:18). So God made us for relationships, for friendships, for companionship.

I can still remember the smile that came over a young woman's face, a couple of years ago, when I said to her that it was OK to want and need a friend, because the Lord made us that way! She had waited to speak to me after our Sunday morning Church Service about how lonely she felt. Her home-life was not the easiest and she had to work while she was studying to help pay for her expenses. So life was busy, demanding, tiring and lonely. She had never realised that she had been created by God not only to live in a quality relationship with him but also with others.

As we talked we looked at how important it is, as a committed follower of Jesus, to relate well to him. We looked at the first eleven verses of John 15, where the Lord Jesus describes a quality relationship with him as a branch drawing its life from the vine. That means that each disciple is to draw his or her life from Jesus by clinging to him. A favourite writer of mine on John's Gospel, Bishop Ryle, paraphrased what the Lord is saying to us in this way:

> Abide in me. Cling to me. Stick fast to me. Live the life of close and intimate communion with me. Get nearer and nearer to me. Roll every burden on me. Cast your whole weight on me. Never let go your hold on me for a moment.

We concluded that this must always be our first priority. However, we also recognised that living in union and communion with the Lord Jesus Christ will never isolate us from people, and our dependence on him will not make us independent of others. As we read from verse twelve through to seventeen, we realised that Jesus commands those who are clinging to him to reach out in relationships with other people. Because twice in six verses he says, 'Love each other.' Therefore to know the Lord Jesus involves not only a vertical relationship with God but also a horizontal one with others, both in his family and outside.

She then said to me, 'That's like the cross.'

'What is?' I asked.

'What we have just said,' she replied. 'The cross points upwards to heaven and reaches out to others; that's how we should live.'

Somehow, something had dropped into her heart that provided the understanding, peace and confidence-builder she needed at that point in her life. We prayed and parted. Today she is living and working in another country and the last time I heard was still reaching up to God and out to others.

Sometimes we fall into the trap of thinking that the Lord is only interested in 'spiritual' matters and not with other issues, such as friendship and loneliness. The truth is that the Lord Jesus Christ died, not only to restore our relationship with God, but also to heal our relationships with other people. It is both amazing and important to discover the large role friendship played in the lives of the men God used in the Bible.

Moses had both an Aaron and a Joshua to support him; David had many loyal friends, but in particular Jonathan; Daniel, who expressed real faith in God, was supported by three friends; the

Lord Jesus chose twelve disciples 'to be with him'; John and Peter and James had special times with the Lord; Paul constantly related to a number of intimate friends, and as he faced death, he urged Timothy, 'Do your best to come to me quickly . . . only Luke is with me.'

The fact that these servants of God needed others, underlines the vital need we all have to establish strong and satisfying friendships that not only meet our needs but educate and equip us to meet the needs of others as well. Because not only does everybody need a friend, but everybody can be a friend. The writer of the apocryphal book *Sirach*, expressed real wisdom when he wrote, 'A faithful friend is a strong shelter; the man who finds one has found a treasure.'

Doctor Luke says 'Jesus grew'. We now know that originally it meant 'making one's way forward by pushing aside obstacles' and that it was a nautical and military metaphor. He goes on to tell us that Jesus grew 'in favour with God and man'. In other words he grew spiritually and socially. He had quality relationships with his Father above and people around him.

Jesus grew spiritually

Early Christians gave Jesus the title *Archegos*. It does not have a one word equivalent in English. It describes someone who leads, and through his

41

leadership stirs others into activity and brings them with him. It was used in classical Greek to describe the heroes who founded great cities. The Founder was not only the person who began it but the person whose example was meant to serve as a model and stimulus for the inhabitants in years to come.

Jesus, Peter tells us, is the 'Archegos of life' (Acts 3:15). The author of the book of Hebrews tells us that Jesus is the Author (Archegos) and the Pioneer (Archegos) of our faith and salvation (Hebrews 12:2; 2:10).

Picture a group of soldiers being led by their captain through a jungle during a battle. He leads his men by first of all facing the dangers and difficulties himself. He 'cuts a path' or 'blazes a trail' so that his men can follow.

Jesus is the great trail-blazer. He is the Captain of our salvation and has gone through what we are going through. Now he tells us, 'Follow me.' We know so little about Jesus' life as a child. His home was presumably the typical flat-roofed, one-roomed house of the time, built of clay. Joseph probably worked from home making agricultural tools with perhaps some furniture and building projects as extras.

In spite of the relative simplicity of home, Jesus seems to have had a good education. He was invited, for example, to read the Old Testament in

Hebrew in the synagogue at Nazareth. Not every person of his age could read Hebrew, even though they may have been able to speak in that language. At that time, Jewish boys were normally educated in the local synagogue.

Nazareth, where he grew up, was a part of Galilee. It was often called 'Galilee of the Gentiles' because of the large number of non-Jews living there. The great roads that brought traders from the east and Roman soldiers from the west passed through Galilee. In his home town, Jesus would meet and mix with many people who were not Jewish. He would be able to speak more than one language. He could speak and read Hebrew; however, the language he would use at home and among his friends would be Aramaic. He probably spoke Greek as well, for that was the international language used throughout the Roman Empire.

In the midst of a simple upbringing, an ordinary education and an unknown, insignificant town, Jesus grew in favour with God. He lived for God's smile!

Luke's description of Jesus' adolescence is short, simple and yet profound. That makes me wonder whether the one story he tells us about Jesus as a boy in the Temple, is an illustration of what he describes.

When Jesus was twelve years old he accompanied his parents to Jerusalem for the annual

Passover Festival, which they attended each year.

After the celebration was over they set off home to Nazareth, but Jesus stayed behind in Jerusalem. His parents didn't miss him the first day, for they assumed he was with their friends and relatives. When they couldn't find him, they went back to Jerusalem to search for him there.

It was not through carelessness that they did not miss him. A Jewish boy became a man when he was twelve years of age. So, Jesus for the first time went to the Passover. Usually the women among the travellers started out a lot earlier than the men, for they travelled more slowly. Normally the younger children accompanied them. The men started later and travelled faster and the two groups wouldn't meet until the evening campsite was reached.

No doubt Joseph thought Jesus was with Mary and Mary thought he would now be travelling with the men and so it was not until the evening camp that they missed him. Three days later they finally discovered him. He was in the Temple, sitting among the teachers of the Law, discussing deep questions with them and amazing everybody with his understanding and answers. His parents didn't know what to think.

'Hearing and asking questions' is a normal Jewish phrase describing a student learning from his teachers. So Jesus was listening to the discussions and eagerly searching for knowledge and understanding like an avid student. The discussion that takes place between Jesus and his parents at this point is a mega moment in his life.

> 'My son, why have you done this to us? Your father and I have been terribly worried trying to find you.'
>
> He answered them, 'Why did you have to look for me? Didn't you know that I had to be in my Father's house?' But they did not understand his answer.
>
> So Jesus went back with them to Nazareth, where he was obedient to them. His mother treasured all these things in her heart. Jesus grew both in body and wisdom, gaining favour with God and men. (Luke 2:48b-52, G.N.B.)

Jesus very definitely but gently takes the name 'Father' and gives it to God! Somehow, somewhere, sometime he must have discovered his own unique relationship to God; and now describes God as 'my Father'. Jesus discovered who he was!

It is obvious from the story that the discovery and the declaration didn't make him arrogant, exclusive or big-headed. Because he went back home with his parents and was 'obedient to them'. Jesus continues to develop quality relationships with his Father above and his parents beside him.

It was World War 1. They had enlisted together,

trained together, were posted together and fought together in the trenches. During an attack, one of them was critically wounded in a field littered with barbed wire and was unable to move. The whole area was still under crossfire and to try and reach him was to enter a death trap. His friend decided to try.

Before he could get out of his own trench, his sergeant hauled him back inside and ordered him to stay. 'It's too late. You can't do him any good, and you'll only get yourself killed.'

Some minutes later, the officer turned and moved up the trench. Instantly the man was out of the trench, into the field after his friend. A few minutes went by, he staggered back, mortally wounded, with his dead friend in his arms.

His sergeant was furious. 'What a waste. He's dead and you soon will be, it wasn't worth it.'

'Yes, it was, sarg. When I got to him, he only said one thing and then he died. It was, "I knew you'd come!"'

'A friend loves at all times' (Proverbs 17:17).

Prayer

Dear Father,
I thank you that you created me to know you and enjoy a quality relationship with you and others around me.

Thank you for providing Jesus for me. Not only to die for me but also to live for me.

Thank you that through the Holy Spirit living in me, I can draw on his strength and gifts to follow the example that Jesus is for me.

In Jesus' Name,
Amen.

Questions

1. Do I choose people as friends because of my needs or because of their needs?

2. What change could take place to improve the quality of my relationship with God?

SO WHAT'S NEXT?

People
Under
Pressure

Part
2

Barrels, Bricks
And Solo-sex

Chapter 5

Tough times. We all have them. Some are worse than others. Like the one the building-site worker had when he tried to be helpful. This story, I believe, appeared on an accident form:

'When I got to the building I found that the hurricane had knocked off some bricks around the top. So I rigged up a beam with a pulley at the top of the building and hoisted up two barrels full of bricks. When I had fixed the damaged area, there were a lot of bricks left over. I went to the bottom and began releasing the line. Unfortunately, the barrel of bricks was much heavier than I was - and before I knew the barrel started coming down, jerking me up.

I decided to hang on since I was too far off the ground by then to jump, and half-way up I met the barrel of bricks coming down fast. I got a hard blow on my shoulder. I continued to the top, banging my head against the beam and getting my fingers pinched and jammed in the pulley. The barrel hit the ground, burst its bottom and the bricks spilled out.

I was now heavier than the barrel. I started down again at high speed. Halfway, I met the barrel coming up fast and received severe injuries to my shins. When I hit the ground, I landed on the pile of spilled bricks, sustaining painful cuts and deep bruises. I let go of my grip of the line. The barrel came down fast - giving me another blow on my head and I ended up in hospital.

I respectfully request sick leave.'

I'm sure he did!

Because we are people in process, we are by definition people under pressure. The changes we go through in this period of growth to maturity sometimes hit us like barrels or cut us like those bricks.

Take for example *the social structures of your parents.* You were born without being consulted. You couldn't pick your family. You arrived dependant. Immediately social structures were built around you which your parents decided for you. They gave you their values, imposed their controls, provided for you; as a result gave you a sense of security.

As you grow up, another factor comes into play: *the social attraction of your peers*. It's scary, but you don't want to be with your parents. You don't want to be seen shopping with your mum. Going on holiday with them is like going into a contaminated zone, sitting in church with them is just not on.

What's happening? Something is more important to you than parents - your peers. This then brings us into contact with *the social challenges of the opposite sex*.

There was a time when you didn't know that there was such a thing as 'the opposite sex'. In fact, at times they were to be detested. But then something happened. That gangly little creep from down the road or across the classroom, who used to have braces and zits changed! The first 'love affair' begins, you get all torn up inside and sometimes you get hurt.

'In process' and 'under pressure' seem to go together. Everybody goes through their tough times - it's normal. These changes and challenges are all taking place within the context of our society.

Here is a small fact-file on some aspects of our society in the United Kingdom:

* More than 1 in 3 marriages will now end in divorce; more than half of those while the couple still have a child under sixteen. It is predicted that by the year 2000, 3 million people will go through divorce.

* By sixteen, 30% live with only one natural parent; in most situations, with the mother.

* Almost half of all British girls have sex before their sixteenth birthday.

* In 1961, 12% of households were single; in 1988, 26% of households have people living on their own, either because of divorce, bereavement or not marrying.

* By 1983 over two million legal abortions had been performed since Sir David Steel's 1967 abortion act was passed.

* Consumer credit rose by 300% between 1982 - 89 to 45.4 billion pounds.

* 1 in 8 children and young people, aged 7 - 15 claim to drink alcohol regularly.

* 1 in 3 children and young people aged between 11-15 work outside school hours in jobs that breach the laws governing the hours they may work.

It's facts like these that hit us like barrels and cut us like those bricks. Barrels and bruises are part of all of our lives because they are part of living in the real world. So is sex.

Our society, so it would seem, is obsessed with sex. Most popular magazines, modern films, numerous television programmes, many commercial adverts and parts of the music industry are blatantly designed to arouse and 'play on' our sexual urges and desires.

God is pro-sex

The more I dig into the Bible, the more convinced I become that the God of all the Earth is pro-sex. If you are looking for anti-sex information or ammunition, you will not find it in God's Book. God created it and Paul reminds us:

> Everything that God has created is good; nothing is to be rejected, but everything is to be received with a prayer of thanks . . . (1 Timothy 4:4 G.N.B.)

Or as David expresses it:

> You made all the delicate, inner parts of my body, and knit them together in my mother's womb. Thank you for making me so wonderfully complex! It is amazing to think about. Your workmanship is marvellous . . . You were there while I was being formed in utter seclusion! (Psalm 139: 13-15 Living Bible)

The Bible is never anti-sex. You will find nothing negative in it about the act of sexual intercourse itself. In fact, its language in describing the sex act is extravagant and views it as a celebration.

What God's Word does insist on is sexual intercourse in the relationship for which it was designed: marriage. Someone once said that intercourse is God's wedding present for married couples, to be unwrapped on the wedding night within the commitment of marriage.

Adultery, promiscuity, lust, homosexuality
The Bible uses four words to describe sexual intercourse outside of marriage.

* Adultery: intercourse between a married person and someone to whom that person is not married.

> You shall not commit adultery (Exodus 20:14; Deuteronomy 5:18; Matthew 19:18; Romans 13:9).

* Promiscuity: The Bible has also something to say about casual sex. The modern translations use the term 'sexual immorality' to translate the older word 'fornication'. Fornication is sexual/genital intercourse with someone to whom you are not married.

The body is not meant for sexual immorality, but for the Lord (1 Corinthians 6:13 N.I.V.).

Flee from sexual immorality (1 Corinthians 6:18 N.I.V.).

* Lust: Jesus goes even further and says,

But I tell you that anyone who looks at a woman lustfully has already committed adultery with her in his heart (Matthew 5:28 N.I.V.).

To lust means to dwell on the desire for someone's body, to feed on that desire, to give in to inappropriate desires by stealing what is not yours to take.

* Homosexuality: Sexual relations with a person of the same sex. There are seven references to homosexuality in the Bible: Genesis 19:1-11; Leviticus 18:22; Leviticus 20:13; Judges 19:22-25; Romans 1:26-27; 1 Corinthians 6:9; 1 Timothy 1:9-11.

Do you not know that the wicked will not inherit the kingdom of God? Do not be deceived: Neither the sexually immoral . . . nor adulterers nor male prostitutes nor homosexual offenders . . . will inherit the kingdom of God (1 Corinthians 6:9-10 N.I.V.).

This strong language is typical of the Bible's attitude to homosexual genital activity.

From God's point of view, sex is good! His context for its expression and enjoyment is marriage. For marriage, as he planned it, means commitment, permanence and faithfulness. Sexual intercourse in that context is the intimate expression of that commitment of love. In fact, Jesus says that it is so deep a commitment, so permanent a love, that the two become one flesh.

When I went to school I was taught that one plus one equalled two. Jesus says that in marriage, one plus one equals one!! In the context of marriage and sexual union, heaven's arithmetic is different from that of planet earth.

When Jesus spoke about two becoming one, he was talking about something that involves more than sexual intimacy. He was meaning that the two become one in every area of their lives and the sex act is the pinnacle of their oneness.

Sex outside of marriage is a living lie because it divorces one aspect of marriage from all the others of which it speaks. As two people surrender and join their bodies, they have surrendered and joined themselves. For in giving their bodies they are giving themselves. Sex outside of marriage is an action without reality and therefore in the act I am projecting a lie.

Take some hydrogen and oxygen and put these

two colourless, odourless gases together. Pass an electrical charge through them. If you don't know what you are doing you will have an explosion. If you do know what you are doing, you will finish up with a liquid called water: H_2O. A different, new and fuller entity has been made.

In Christian marriage two people come with all their qualities, gifts and uniqueness and are fused into one. Somehow, through the 'leaving and the cleaving', the promises and commitments made in the wedding ceremony, the fusing of bodies in genital intercourse, God gives the electric charge of His blessing and oneness is the result. God joins them together.

Two people turn from their singleness (they leave) and turn to each other (they cleave).

Did you know that the Greek word for cleave is glue? I suppose you could say God sticks them together!! I can almost hear one say to the other, "I'm stuck to you and you are stuck to me!"

This is God's idea and God's formula!

A few weeks ago I spent five days with one hundred young people. It was a superb time. Loads of activities, lots of laughs, plenty food, late nights, brilliant music and some serious Bible study and discussion all added up to a significant five day wonder.

About two and a half days into the event, a small

but steady stream of guys started making their quiet way to talk to me about you know what. Their basic question was about the issue that if God's framework for our lives rules out pre-marital intercourse, where do we draw the line on our sexual expression and experience.

You are not a robot

One of the young men complained about God. He basically said, "I've given my life to God, so why does he allow me to give in to temptation so much?"

The real problem was that he was putting himself in situations of temptation where he knew that the temptation would overcome his flabby will. He was reading magazines, watching certain videos and dating so many girls that he was feeding his weakness in this area.

"Why blame God?" I said. "God isn't going to handcuff your hands or chain you to the kitchen sink or imprison your imagination. You are not a robot!"

God has made you with a freedom to choose to make good choices or bad ones. The choice to obey or disobey the Lord is yours.

Masturbation ('you know what')

Masturbation is the stimulation of one's own genitals to the point of orgasm. It is a very common form of sexual arousal outside of marriage.

Research generally concludes that about 95% of all males and a lower percentage (50%-90%) of all females have masturbated to the point of orgasm at least some time in their lives. The frequency of it declines after adolescence and marriage, but it does not disappear. Apparently most married men and many married women continue this practice throughout their lives - and regular church attenders masturbate as much as non-attenders.

I've spoken to a number of Christian counsellors on this subject and this is a summary of the information and wisdom that I've collected so far:

* Masturbation is very common and does no harm physically.

* It is never mentioned in the Bible. This does not make it right, but it does show that masturbation is not a major sin - otherwise God's Word would have mentioned it.

* It can be helpful in relieving sexual or other tensions.
* Christian counsellors have differing views on it. It has been described as 'sin', 'no big deal on God's list of priorities', 'a safety-valve given by God'.

* It can produce some harmful influences e.g. guilt. It can be an escape from loneliness into a world of fantasy. It can encourage self-centredness and lower self-esteem.

It can feed and be fed by lust - in that context it clearly is wrong.

* It can be reduced by prayer, a genuine willingness to allow God the Holy Spirit to control your sexual appetite, an avoiding of sexually arousing material and wise petting in the course of dating.

* Any person who speaks or writes about masturbation is going to be criticised!

I think that it is a sin when it is accompanied by a lust for sexual relations which God forbids, when it controls us and when it spoils and hinders our relationship with Jesus.

Masturbators must know that other people accept them, that the Lord helps and forgives when it is sin and that talking openly about it helps to deflate the pressure that it brings on people.

I agree with David Seamands who wrote:

When there is open communication on the subject of sex, including masturbation . . . it will . . . not become a major problem . . . It's high time we stopped making such a "big deal" out of masturbation and give it the well-deserved unimportance it merits. (David A. Seamands: 'Sex, Inside and Outside of Marriage' in *The Secrets of our Sexuality* Word 1976; p. 156)

Prayer

Dear Father,

Help me to see and understand myself from your perspective. Help me to know when it is the world and not your Word that is shaping my thoughts and attitudes and dominating my choices. Help me to choose to obey and not the opposite. Help me to please you in my sexuality.

In Jesus' Name,
Amen.

Question

As a result of what you have read in this chapter: describe your attitude to sex; pray about God changing an area of your life sexually that may be hurting him; what can you do to deal with a temptation you face regularly?

1. Attitude:

2. Prayer:

3. Change:

Doorways
To
Danger

Chapter 6

It was a mid-week Bible study night in a local church and I was about half-way through my message, when I saw a young man move physically on his seat in a way that was unusual and noticeable. His head was angled at an odd position, his eyes were strange and he appeared to be reacting to and opposing what I was saying. During a prayer time at the end of the teaching, he was helped to a separate room.

After the Bible Study was officially over, I was asked to talk with the young man. As I entered the room and approached him he reacted violently and loudly and his voice changed. He pranced around the room shouting, swearing, punching the walls and kicking the furniture.

I soon realised that I had met, in an open confrontation, for the first time in my life, a demon! It laughed at me, mocked me, hurled insults and abuse at me.

After one hour of reading the Scriptures out loud, having others join me to pray and together listening to the Lord for guidance, it was time to act. Having silenced the demon in the name and power of the Lord Jesus Christ, I then commanded it to leave the young man it was oppressing and hurting.

I will not forget the physical heaving and shaking, along with the vulgar language that was then expressed as the evil spirit obeyed the Lord Jesus and left the young man. As he slouched backward, we then continued to pray that the Lord would give him peace, protection and renewal of strength.

On my way home that night I realised as I had never done before that not only are demons real, but, Jesus Christ is Lord!

That experience launched me into reading the four Gospels again to see what Jesus said and did to demons when he encountered them. It also made me read lots of other material on the subject. In the course of my research, I came across a statement by an old writer called Henry Law. He described the devil's activity in these words:

He never slumbers, never is weary, never relents, never abandons hope. He deals his blows alike at childhood's weakness, youth's inexperience, manhood's strength, and the totterings of age. He watches to ensnare the morning thought, he departs not with the shades of night . . . he enters the palace, the hut, the fortress, the camp, the fleet. He invades every chamber of every dwelling, every pew of every sanctuary. He is busy with the busy. He hurries about with the active. He sits by each bed of sickness and whispers into each dying ear. As the spirit quits the tenement of clay, he still draws his bow with unrelenting rage.

It seems to me that those words are more true now at the end of the 20th century than when they were first spoken.

Not too long ago, the devil's doings were kept pretty much below the surface in society. Now all that has changed. A widespread and intense interest in occult powers and practices confronts us everywhere. School and college students use ouija boards and tarot cards seriously. Sophisticated and wealthy people attend seances. Popular magazines feature articles about black and white magic and highlight the lives of well-known seers. Newspapers and TV provide daily astrology readings and coverage of cults that worship Satan. Social workers have to deal with children who have been sexually abused in acts of Satan worship. Less than three miles from where I am writing this book, (in north west England), children in a junior school, were dabbling to such an extent in the occult, that the staff banned certain activities during break times because of the disturbance and fear that was being created in the school.

Occult practices

The word 'occult' comes from the Latin word 'occultus' and simply means 'hidden, secret or dark'. It is the word used to describe those phenomena which transcend, or appear to transcend, the world of the senses. 'Occult practices' are experiences that bring a person into contact with 'spirits' that are demonic in source. Such contact is forbidden by God. These contacts may be produced by mechanical means e.g. ouija board or tarot cards; or by consultation with a person, e.g. medium, fortune-teller, clairvoyant.

We are often warned in God's Word about the spirit world. As never before we need to listen to and observe what God says:

> Put on all of God's armour so that you will be able to stand safe against all strategies and tricks of Satan. For we are not fighting against people made of flesh and blood, but against persons without bodies - the evil rulers of the unseen world, those mighty satanic beings and great evil princes of darkness who rule this world; and against huge numbers of wicked spirits in the spirit world. (Ephesians 6: 11-12, Living Bible)

Doorways to Danger
The Evangelical Alliance* have produced an excellent video and information pack entitled *Doorways to Danger*. This is how their information pack begins:

> A neighbourhood seance. An astrologer's helpline. Teenagers' fun with ouija boards. These seemingly innocent entertainments could be entrances into a sinister world of evil and destruction.

It then goes on to add that involvement with the supernatural through these kind of doorways is

*Further details can be obtained from The Evangelical Alliance, Whitefield House, 186 Kennington Park Road, London SE11 4BT

inflicting mental, spiritual and physical damage on growing numbers of people, many of them still at school. And seemingly trivial activities such as horoscopes and Halloween parties can be part of the process.

Psychiatrist, Dr. Chris Andrew warns: 'Involvement with the occult can lead to anything from depression and broken relationships to sexual deviation and murder.'

Even those who for fun become involved with astrology, seances and spells risk 'devastating consequences', says former Senior Consultant to the Royal Liverpool Hospital and University of Liverpool, Dr. David Enoch, 'They're unleashing forces into their lives that they don't understand and often can't combat.'

Estimates indicate that there are as many as 30,000 witches in Britain. In Lancashire, where I live, there is a minister who regularly counsels young people caught in the grip of the occult. He believes that there are 30 witches' covens in North East Lancashire alone. He fears that young people are making the journey from the classroom fun of Halloween on to direct involvement in occult practices.

Halloween

'The origins of Halloween lie in the distant past,' says *Doorways to Danger*, when celebrations were held by the Druids in honour of Samhuinn, Lord of the Dead, whose festival fell on 1st November and marked the entry of winter.

It was the Druids' belief that, on the eve of the festival, Samhuinn called together the wicked spirits that within the past 12 months had been condemned to inhabit the bodies of animals.

Today's Halloween with its 'trick or treat' pranks, ghosts and witches' costumes and pumpkin lanterns, seems a far cry from secret rites to appease ancient pagan deities. But that is what lies under the surface.

Ouija boards

A simple device for communicating with outside forces has been likened to inviting a child to build sand castles on a beach laid with land mines.

Unfortunately, there is a craze for this game today even although it has been branded as fearfully dangerous. Together with books on magic and the supernatural it has been the bait on the hook for many young people.

If you are prepared to try and contact forces outside of yourself, then you will do it. That is dangerous and getting hooked is highly dangerous.

Spiritualism

There are around 52,000 spiritualists in Britain

today and their churches and meetings report a 100% growth in attendance in the last five years. It has been described as one of the innocent faces of the occult.

They claim to bring messages from those who have died. However, much that happens can be the result of the medium using intuition, observation or doing some homework on clients before a meeting. In some cases, the unexplained can be attributed to demonic deception with evil spirits sharing actual information about people who have died, even to impersonating their voices.

God doesn't like it

One of the ways that God has made himself known to people is through the Bible.

In the Old Testament he says:

Let no one be found among you who ... practices divination or sorcery, interprets omens, engages in witchcraft, or casts spells, or who is a medium or spiritist or who consults the dead. Anyone who does these things is detestable to the Lord (Deuteronomy 18:10-12 N.I.V.).

Do not turn to mediums or seek out spiritists; for you will be defiled by them. I am the Lord your God (Leviticus 19:31 N.I.V.).

In the New Testament, God says:

> The acts of the sinful nature are . . . witchcraft (Galatians 5:20 N.I.V.).

So, God doesn't like it and says that it is wrong to have anything to do with occult activities. And he warns of the consequences that will follow those who do.

Doorways out of Danger

You may have just realised that you are at risk having been or are involved with some aspect of the occult. There is help available. This is what you should do:

* Pray - which is simply talking to God.

Ask him to help you find freedom from your fears. Ask forgiveness for your involvement in occult practices and renounce your allegiance to them. Ask him to come into your life (if you have never done so.)

Find two or more Christians to pray with you. Soon!

* Action - make a clean break from the aspect of occultism that you have engaged in.

Destroy all reminders that link you with the occult (e.g. books; videos; tarot cards etc.).

Start reading the Bible. Begin with Mark or Luke's Gospel in the New Testament.

Contact a Christian friend and ask for their help and prayers.*

From Witchcraft to Christ

Doreen Irvine in her book, *From Witchcraft to Christ*, tells her story:

> I yearned with all my heart to be pure, to be free, to love and serve Jesus Christ and him alone ... I prayed and thanked the Lord Jesus for setting me free ... but within a short time other demons revealed themselves to me. Some gave names, some didn't. I was in deep despair.

She goes on to tell of her awful situation which continued to torment her and the stickability, commitment and godliness of a Baptist minister, the Rev Arthur Neil:

> My life had been an open door to demon possession. It would be some time before I was completely free, before every demon would depart.
>
> Not that Jesus Christ could not have done it all at once and altogether. He could have. But as I have said before, his ways are past finding out ... Mr. Neil fasted and prayed before each session. He knew he was coming into contact with powers of darkness in an actual genuine way.

*(For further help write to: Contact for Christ (CRO), P.O. Box 150 Bromley, Kent.)

After seven months of this deliverance help in the name of Jesus, according to the Bible and through the power of God's Holy Spirit, she describes one special night in Bristol:

> What a night of rejoicing that was! I was free. Jesus had done it. His mighty power was felt in a tremendous way by one and all. Mr. Neil's face was aglow with the glory of God, and so was mine. Such praise went up in that church, such as was never heard before. It was truly a memorable night. (Doreen Irvine: *From Witchcraft to Christ* Concordia Press, 1973) pp 125, 137

For the kingdom of God is not a matter of words but of power (1 Corinthians 4:20 G.N.B.)

Prayer

Dear Father,
I praise you that you are Almighty God, LORD of Heaven and Earth. I want to spend my life doing your will and fulfilling your purposes.

I want to live my life as an obvious citizen of your kingdom saying in word and deed a big NO to Satan and a huge YES to Jesus.

Forgive all the sins that I have committed. Free me from any area of darkness where your light has not entered.

I offer my life afresh to you. Please fill me with your Holy Spirit so that with your help and guidance I will obey you as my Lord.

In Jesus' Name,
Amen.

Action

Read:
Colossians 1: 15-23
Colossians 2: 6-3:17

UNDER THE INFLUENCE

Chapter 7

I couldn't believe what I was seeing flash across my mind. One of the most explicit sex scenes you could ever imagine!

Where was I? No, I wasn't reading soft porn, in my bedroom, behind a closed door! I was sitting in my blue mini (affectionately known as Bluebell) in front of a red traffic light, on my way home from work. There was no romantic song playing on the radio, no sexy-looking girl crossing in front of me. I was just waiting for the green light, not thinking about anything in particular, when zap! this explicit sex scene flashed across my mind.

It was so clear, fresh and powerful. It surprised and shocked me.

Where did it come from? A film I had watched three or four years earlier and about 150 miles from where I was sitting - that's where!

It amazed me to think that something I had seen so long ago could still be lodged in, rise up and influence me while I was sitting at traffic lights.

By this time a green light had appeared as well as a number of car horns blasting at me to get a move on, so I hurriedly drove off.

When I arrived home, I went quickly inside and fell on my knees, in front of a chair near the fireplace. I asked the Lord to forgive me for my wicked thoughts and desires and for the first time in my life did something I have never regretted.

I gave my mind to the Lord!

I asked Him to rule that area of my life with *His* love, truth, wisdom and power.

Through what had taken place at the traffic lights, I realised that what travels into me through my eyes and ears walks around in my mind and powerfully influences what I think, how I feel and what I do.

So I prayed, 'Lord, take charge of my mind. Teach and show me how to fill it with good things like your thoughts; so I may think, feel and act differently and in a way that pleases you.'

That prayer was prayed approximately fifteen years ago and I know that the Lord has and will continue to answer it in His way and time.

Influenced by what we see and hear

We are being influenced all the time by what we see and hear. Every day, in countless ways we are bombarded with messages, images and information, not only in the entertainment world, but also in the media. We see newspaper headlines, listen to radio, watch television, walk down streets that display boardings and catch buses and trains that carry advertisements.

Someone has described the messages, images and information as part of the 'twentieth-century landscape' that we live in.

It's not all bad

The influence is not all bad. For example, the other

evening my five-and-a-half year old boy and two-and-a-half year old girl, plus myself, saw on television the tragic scenes taking place in Somalia.

As we watched children crying and so obviously unwell, they asked why they were hurting. That led to a good discussion about the plight of that country and in our evening prayers we asked the Lord to help that country and show us as a family how we might help.

During Esther Rantzen's *That's Life* and *Hearts of Gold* programmes, there have been a number of very moving and challenging presentations.

There was the little boy in Liverpool who, in order to save his grandad from drowning, jumped into the freezing cold water at Liverpool Docks to place a rescue ring over him. Having done that, he then clambered back on to their boat, on to the pier and ran barefoot over cobbles, about 500 metres. He jumped in front of an approaching car, stopped it, and the driver phoned on his car phone for an ambulance. Doctors said that if they had been minutes later in getting his grandad out of the water and to hospital, he would have died. It's no wonder that little boy received a 'heart of gold'.

That influences you!

A few weeks ago we watched a young boy visiting, helping, befriending and making meals for an elderly lady who lived near his home.

One day, while in the elderly lady's house making her dinner, someone stole his bike.

He was heartbroken. His family could not afford to replace it and he couldn't visit his elderly friend as often and do as much as he had.

Somehow all of this got the attention of the *That's Life* team, and they not only filmed him caring for this dear lady, but surprised him with a brand-new bike, exactly the same as had been stolen.

As we watched this, our hearts were touched. And I found myself praying, 'Lord, please make me like that little boy'.

Influenced? You bet I was.

That little boy reminded me of Jesus who 'went about doing good'.

Think of how we have been influenced as we have been informed about the famines in Africa, the atrocities of Tienamen Square, the victims of Ceaucescu, the oppressive influence of Communism in Eastern Europe, the developments of the Gulf War, the plight of the Kurds, the massive internal changes in the Soviet Union, the World Cup, the Olympic Games, the economic climate around the world, the freeing of the hostages, the miscarriages of justice in the British Courts, the AIDS epidemic, child abuse, the development of the European Community, the ozone layer, the destruction of the rain forests and the profound influence on the rest of the world.

To say the least, it is not all bad. In fact, the media are not only here and here to stay, but have a significant role to play in our modern world.

It's not all good

We all know, for example, how the advertising world's appeal is so often to greed, pride, self-centredness and self-indulgence.

It tells you what you need to wear if you want to look cool. Unnecessary luxuries are presented to you as essential ingredients of your life.

Semi-nude photographs of women in newspapers and erotic dancing on videos are supposed to be viewed as harmless entertainment.

Television soap operas often celebrate wealth, power and good looks at the expense of relationships being injured and the law of the land or God's moral law being broken.

Before we go any further, please read carefully, and at least twice, what God has to say about our minds.

God says:

'Be careful *how you think*; your *life is shaped* by your *thoughts*' (Proverbs 4:23. GNB).

'...*fill* your *minds* with those things that are good and that deserve praise: things that are true, noble, right, pure, lovely and honourable' (Phil 4:8. GNB).

'Do not conform yourselves to the standards of this world, but let God *transform you inwardly by a complete change of mind. Then* you will be able to know the will of God - what is good and is pleasing to Him and is perfect' (Romans 12:2. GNB).

Easily influenced

We are easily influenced not only because our life is shaped by our thoughts but also because of the power and amount of modern means of communication.

Take adverts for example

We often hear one message over a period of years! The Cadbury's advert is known to millions. Even as you read, I know that I don't have to complete the following statement: 'All because the lady loves...' Millions know about Heineken lager because it has been advertised hundreds and hundreds of times. I wonder if you can finish this well-known phrase: 'Heineken refreshes the parts other...' Last year while I was driving through a city centre in the north-west of England, I saw an advert on a church building noticeboard that read: 'Jesus refreshes parts of your life that other religions don't'. Such is the powerful influence of advertising.

In the last few years, advertisers have begun to use their adverts as mini-soaps. So we now have on-going romance taking place, all because the only thing a particular man and woman have in common is the coffee they drink.

We have also reached a point in advertising when a cigarette advert can carry a government health warning about the power the cigarette has to destroy and kill, and still the advertisers can make the product so appealing.

Take the news for example

A few evenings ago, I got in late from work, everyone was in bed, and after I made a cup of tea I sat down and watched some TV.

The programme I watched is weekly and is based around a TV news channel called Channel 10 News. It was a very interesting programme.

A man was holding hostage a number of his work mates in his office. Obviously the police, fire and ambulance services were all at the scene. Two or three had been shot and the situation was very intense.

In the thick of all this, a cameraman from the TV news station slipped into the building unnoticed. With his camera running, he proceeded upstairs to the level the gunman was on. Moving along the corridor he came to the office where the hostages and gunman were. The gunman was distracted by the cameraman. At that moment, one of the hostages grabbed his rifle. To everyone's surprise the gunman reached into his jacket, pulled out a handgun and shot the hostage who had grabbed his rifle. Having done that he then faced the camera and blew his own brains out.

What followed was a massive, internal argument in the News Station about whether the information captured on camera should be broadcast. Would it be wrong to show it? Is it right? Who decides and how do they decide?

Right now, from all over the world, the offices of News at Ten, the Six O'clock News, Radio 1, the Independent, the Daily Mail are all receiving a mountain of information. Some of it comes by telephone, cable or fax; some by satellite; some through news agencies. All producing a mountain of information.

Decisions are then made about what is and what is not used. How and how much should be used must also be decided. What will be given major coverage? What will go on the front page or be the major headlines seen and heard in the twenty or thirty minute news programme? News editing also involves asking questions about what is important and relevant and will influence the public (you and me). As the editors choose the items, they also arrange them in an order of importance. That order also influences us.

Sometimes they tell untruths. At times the lies are spoken in words. At other times, the untruth comes through a photograph that has been 'adjusted' for the occasion.

What we must realise is that while we are being informed we are also being influenced.

Take soaps for example

I've been told that the British spend 80 million man-hours a week watching TV soap opera.

It is a powerful and extremely popular medium of entertainment that is not all bad, nor is it all good.

Just as there are many layers to an onion so there are many layers with many meanings in soaps like *Neighbours, EastEnders, Families, Coronation Street, Dallas* and *Brookside*.

They communicate values, routes to happiness and success, relationship skills, certain angles on family life, how to handle difficult situations and people.

We must be more aware that while we are being entertained, informed or targeted by a company selling a product, we are being influenced.

As I'm writing I can hear, in my mind, Cliff Richard singing a line from a song on his *Walking in the Light* album, which goes something like this: 'We are under the influence of somebody all of the time'.

In this almost-21st century world that is so media-saturated, advert-pushing and soap-bubbling we have to be very alert to this truth that not only are we 'under the influence of somebody all of the time', but we can also influence our world as Jesus told us to by being salt and light, in the decay and darkness.

So don't just be a sponge that simply absorbs all you see and hear. Think about the influence the information and entertainment you receive is having on you. Question the values, goals, relationship-styles, perspectives and impact what you see and hear is having on you. Ask the Lord to give you wisdom and discernment and make you a vehicle of His righteousness, justice, truth, love and wisdom in your domestic, local, regional, national and international world.

Prayer

Dear Father
Help me to remember that I'm under the influence of somebody all of the time.

Teach and show me how to be your vehicle of influence where I live, study and work and relax.

Amen.

Questions

1. What soaps, adverts and news programmes are influencing you?

2. If they are not all bad or all good, highlight some of the good and some of the bad influences they have on you.

3. To whom could you be an influence for God and for good; and how and when?

Things
Happen
To Us

Chapter 8

I was standing on the pavement with my friends from our street, when out of her front doorway walked her dad carrying a white coffin. It was a sad moment in our childhood and we all cried.

She was our friend. She was only six or seven. She had died. She was gone from us for ever. We would miss her.

It was early and still dark. The wind was blowing, the rain falling and I ran from where I parked my bike, into the newsagents to collect the newspapers I delivered each morning. Monday mornings are tough, but this one was to be extra tough.

The headline caught my attention. I knew his name. I recognised his face. He was from my Bible group. He had been found, dying from a drugs overdose, on the back seat of a car in a fishing town on the east coast of Scotland. He came from a Christian family. He was one of the older young people in the group and I looked up to him.

She was seventeen. It was four o'clock and she was walking home on her normal route from sixth form college. As she went through the park, a stranger approached her.

He wanted to date her. She refused. He drew a knife and stabbed her through the stomach and liver and then ran. She staggered home bleeding badly. Nobody stopped to help. She was rushed to hospital and underwent immediate surgery. She is a follower of Jesus.

Things happen to us and around us that we do not like, want or understand. Following Christ does not mean we escape tough experiences or tests. In fact, following him is certain to take us into circumstances that may be uncomfortable, painful, stretching, challenging, rewarding, maturing, and faith-building.

It was Malcolm Muggeridge in his book *A Twentieth Century Testimony* who said these wise words:

> Contrary to what might be expected, I look back on my experiences that at the time seemed especially desolating and painful with particular satisfaction. Indeed, I can say with complete truthfulness that everything that I have learned in my 75 years in this world, everything that has truly enhanced and enlightened my experience, has been through affliction and not through happiness.

Not every question gets answered. Not every problem is solved. Not every prayer is answered (the way we want); not every wound is healed.

700 years before the birth of Christ, Isaiah the prophet recorded something the LORD said:

> "My thoughts," says the Lord, "are not like yours, and my ways are different from yours.
>
> As high as the heavens are above the earth,
> So high are my ways and thoughts above yours"
> (Isaiah 55:8-9 G.N.B.).

Philippians

The Philippian church had discovered that the apostle Paul was in prison and they sent Epaphroditus with a gift for him. Paul writes a thank you letter back to them and we have it in the New Testament under the title Philippians.

You would never guess that he is writing from a dark, damp, rat-infested smelly prison. His letter is so positive. In fact he talks about joy eleven times in four chapters.

What Paul believed

He firmly believes that things could only happen to him if God permits them to happen. As a follower of Jesus, he was convinced that God would not permit meaningless things to happen to him, so he looked for God's purpose in all that took place.

As my friend, Stuart Briscoe says, 'Paul had discovered that things happen to him in order that things should happen in him. And things happened in him so that things could happen through him.'

Paul writes in chapter 1:12:

I want you to know . . . that *the things that have happened to me* have really helped. (G.N.B.)

What kind of things had happened to him?

Uncomfortable things

This man has a brilliant mind. He had been taught in the best universities of his day and has reached a high academic status. He also has remarkable leadership ability and is demonstrating that in his position as an apostle. In his living and lifestyle he has sacrificed so much for the Lord Jesus and now he is in prison (in chains). (See chapter 1:7,13,14,17).

Frustrating things

He was a man of action and a man with a mission. There was so much for him to do, places to go and people to meet. His journeys, mostly on foot, took him in excess of 6000 miles. And now his feet are in chains. This man is going nowhere fast.

Disappointing things

Some people, who claim to be followers of Christ, are behaving in such a way that they are trying to create more trouble for him while he is in prison (see chapter 1:14-17). Unfortunately, some of his opponents are members of the same team.

So things are happening to him that are uncomfortable, frustrating and disappointing. And these are happening, not because he is disobedient to Christ, but because he is living to please Christ. It's his obedience that has taken him into these circumstances.

While these things were happening to him God

was at work in him. You can see that in his attitudes and reactions to his problems, God and death.

Problems

It appears that he saw his problems in the right way and kept them to their proper size. It is so easy to be overwhelmed by your problems; sometimes to the point where you worship and bow down to them. That's the point when your problems are in charge of you. At other times, we ignore them and pretend they don't exist. Paul is facing the problem of where he is, what it's like, why he is there and when will it be different. His attitude is so different. (Read chapter 1:15-18). This is because his problem has become a platform on which he can discover God's presence and his purpose.

During January 1990, I was reading Corrie Ten Boom's book *Tramp for the Lord*. In it she recalls how God looked after her and her sister Betsy in a German concentration camp. Having smuggled her Bible into the camp she would read it in an over-crowded, lice-infested bed.

One night she read Psalm 32:8, which says: 'I will teach you and guide you in the way you should go. I will keep you under my eye.' As she thought carefully about what that verse says, the Lord whispered through her thoughts that he doesn't have problems, only plans for our lives. For he *teaches and guides us* in *the way* we should go.

Paul realised that the prison problem he was going through was somehow or other part of God teaching and guiding him in the way he should go. So it was a plan not primarily a problem.

God

At the beginning of 1990 I was really struggling with almost every part of my life. Early one morning during my morning prayers, I cried out to God in a desperate way. The Bible was just black ink on white paper. Prayer was like talking to the ceiling. I desperately needed to hear from God. As a final act, I put on a praise tape. The first song was based on the words of Philippians chapter 1: 6. This is how that verse reads:

> And so I am sure that God, who began this good work in you, will carry it on until it is finished on the Day of Christ Jesus.

The song basically went something like this:

> If the struggle you're facing is slowly replacing your hope with despair;
> or the process is long and you're losing your song in the night.
> You can be sure that the Lord has his hand on you, safe and secure he will never abandon you;
> You are his treasure and he finds his pleasure in you.
> He who began a good work in you will be faithful to complete it in you.

I began to see that Paul the apostle not only got his problems into perspective, he also developed a healthy and proper view of God.

He realised that God finishes as well as begins his work in our lives. So in this very uncomfortable, frustrating and disappointing situation, his attitude to God is one of trust. He can depend on God to help him. He believes that through the prayers of God's people and the help which comes from the Holy Spirit, ultimately he will be OK (see chapter 1:18-21).

Death

He has also discovered that the only certainty in life is death. Added to that is the belief that to die is not loss but gain. He is thoroughly convinced that death for the follower of Jesus is not a step into inky blackness, but one that takes us into the radiant presence of Jesus for ever and ever. And to be with Christ is 'a far better thing.' (See chapter 1:21-26)

Horrendous things may be happening to this man but wonderful things are happening in him.

Over many years I have prayed to God to give me links and friendships with older and godly people. He has answered beyond my asking. Probably the longest and fondest is Alec and Jean Easton in Grangemouth. Alec has many wise sayings. As I've been writing this chapter, one in particular has been coming to mind again and again. It goes like this:

> God has a greater work to do in us than through us;
> but the greater the work he does in us, the greater
> will be the work through us.

And this seems to be true in the life of the apostle Paul. God seized him as he was travelling to Damascus to capture Christians. He had been fighting with God like an ox kicking against its owner's stick. But the Lord won the battle and Paul surrendered his heart and will to King Jesus. (Read Acts 26:12-23). God certainly had a big job to do in him. He also had a great work to do through him. Listen to what Jesus said to him that day on the Damascus road:

> I have appeared to you to appoint you as my servant.
> You are to tell others what you have seen of me today
> and what I will show you in the future . . . You are to
> open their eyes and turn them from the darkness to
> the light and from the power of Satan to God, so that
> through their faith in me they will have their sins
> forgiven and receive their place among God's cho-
> sen people (Acts 26:16-18 G.N.B.)

Not bad for a job description, don't you think? I don't think that would appear in job centres! This was the big job that God had to do through him. And even when he was in prison, chained 24 hours per day, isolated from his family and apparently going nowhere fast, great things were happening through him.

What's happening through him?

He says in chapter 1:12 that the things that have happened to him have really helped the progress of the gospel. As a result of his imprisonment, the whole palace guard have heard the good news about Jesus.

The palace guard were ten thousand selected troops who served for twelve to sixteen years. Ultimately they became the Emperor's private body guard. Paul was chained to one of them day and night; so he found himself talking about Christ to the finest regiment in the Roman army.

Imagine it. The prisoner becomes the teacher while the soldiers become the students. All over Caesar's court the talk is about Paul and his good news! It's no wonder he uses the word 'progress'. It literally means 'cutting away undergrowth' or 'removing barriers which would hinder the progress of an army.' That's what's happening through him inside the prison.

Outside, Christians are gaining confidence in the Lord so that they grow bolder in preaching God's message. Added to all that is the letter of Philippians itself which we have in our Bibles today.

Perhaps it's because of the incredible things that happened to him that what he says in verse 29 has such impact. It reads like this: 'For you have been given the privilege of serving Christ, not only by believing in him, but also by suffering for him' (G.N.B.). 'Given' is a word that means 'a gift of grace.' He is reminding God's people in Philippi that serving Christ is a gift which will not only involve trusting Christ but also suffering for Christ.

Sharon is fifteen. A few weeks ago, during a class of social ethics at school, she was looking at the lyrics of the John Lennon song *Imagine*. The whole class had been asked to underline the positive and negative statements in the song.

Part of the song says, 'imagine there is no heaven' and Sharon, who is a Christian, felt this was a negative statement.

Her teacher, who is aware of Sharon's faith, only looked at hers, and began to talk about heaven. In a rather patronising way she proceeded to say that it's only when you are little that you think of heaven as a place. And when you grow up you realise that it is a state of mind. She then turned on Sharon and quizzed her about what she believed about heaven. The teacher did this in such a way that the whole class turned on her.

The pressure not only went on all day, but the debate spread through the whole school. Some mocked her, others laughed, a good number asked serious questions about heaven and hell.

For Sharon it was painful and difficult. However, it forced her to stand up and speak out for what she believes. It made her think more deeply about heaven. It caused her to pray more strongly and specifically. And lots of people heard some parts of God's message.

At fifteen she has begun to discover that things happen to us so that things can happen in us. And things happen in us in order that things will happen through us.

How about you?

Prayer

Dear Father,
It's good to discover that you will not permit meaningless things to happen to me. Help me to remember this and look out for and pray for your divine purpose in my life.

Activate your Holy Spirit in me so that your will gets done in me and through me.

Thank you for the gift and privilege of serving Christ. Help me to understand, appreciate and remember that this involves suffering as well as trusting you more and more day by day.

Your humble and happy servant,
Amen!

Questions

(1) Summarise in no more than three sentences what is happening *to* you just now or during the last six months.

(2) Describe in an honest way what's been happening *in* you.

(3) Name the attitudes that you know the Lord has produced in you and the ones you would like him to change.

(a)

(b)

(c)

(d)

(e)

(f)

People
With
Potential

Part
3

Seize
The
Day

Chapter 9

Not many people read Ecclesiastes these days. But at the end of that forgotten book is one of my favourite chapters in the Bible. This is some of the advice it gives to young people:

'Young people, enjoy your youth. Be happy while you are still young. Do what you want to do, and follow your heart's desire. But remember that God is going to judge you for whatever you do.

Don't let anything worry you or cause you pain. You aren't going to be young very long.

So remember your Creator while you are still young, before those dismal days and years come when you will say, "I don't enjoy life." ' (Ecclesiastes 11: 9-12:1 G.N.B.)

What it's saying here is this: as a young person, you've got so much potential and while you are young, going through this process, experiencing these pressures, remember that you were created for something. Because the time will come when you will be so old that you won't be able to do much anyway. So the time to be what you were created for is when you are young.

Chapter twelve goes on to describe what it's like when you get so old and decrepit that you can't be what you were created to be. It's written in poetry form, sounds a bit weird but is really funny.

'Your arms that have protected you, will tremble, and your legs now strong, will grow weak. Your teeth will be too few to chew your food, and your eyes too dim to see clearly. Your ears will be deaf to the noise of the street. You will barely be able to hear the mill as it grinds or music as it plays, but even the song of a bird will wake you from sleep. You will be afraid of high places, and walking will be dangerous. Your hair will turn white; you will hardly be able to drag yourself along, and all desire will have gone.' (3-5 G.N.B.)

What a picture. Trembling arms, shaky legs, teeth falling out, needing binoculars to see out the front window, can't hear the difference between a police car's siren and a sparrow, afraid of aeroplanes and unable to have sex. That's what it says. 'All desire will have gone.'

What's the point of all this? Well the point is, don't wait until you get to this stage of your life to be what you were created to be. Realise when you are young, that you were created to be and do something and get on with it. Don't wait until it's too late. Seize the day.

What follows in verse six are some pictures which highlight this in a powerful way.

'The silver chain will snap, and the golden lamp will fall and break; the rope at the well will break, and the water jar will be shattered' (G.N.B.)

In those days, they had golden bowls full of oil that they lit and suspended on a silver chain from the ceiling. After a while the silver chain or cord would break, the golden lamp would fall, the oil would spill and the light would go out. That's what our life is like. When we are young we have a strong silver chain and a bright shiny bowl that's full of all kinds of dreams, ideas and enthusiasm and God can set it alight and do something. Don't wait until the chain snaps and the oil is spilt.

The rope at the well is able to pull the bucket up no problem at all when it's new and young. The water jar is a nice shape with lovely colours and doesn't drip when it's being carried to satisfy thirsty people. The time comes, however, when the rope wears thin and the jar cracks and leaks and you lose more than you can deliver. That's what will happen to us. When we are young we can pull and carry and do some good to others. One day however, the rope will break and the jar of our life will be shattered.

So remember your Creator while you are still young and seize the day!

Daniel

I grew up in a small fishing town in Scotland. As a little boy I regularly attended Sunday school. Through that and the Christian family I grew up in, I learned to love the stories of the Bible. One of my

favourites was Daniel. I can still remember a song
we used to sing about him. I think it went something like this:

Dare to be a Daniel
Dare to stand alone
Dare to have a purpose firm
Dare to make it known.

That song captures some of the outstanding
features of his life. It's obvious from the book
called Daniel in the Bible, that he remembered his
Creator while he was still young and seized that
day! Over the years there are certain things about
Daniel that have impressed and influenced me.
For example.

He made up his mind

King Jehoiakim of Judah had been captured by
King Nebuchadnezzar of Babylon when he had
attacked Jerusalem. King Nebuchadnezzar seized
some of the Temple treasures and took some
prisoners back with him to Babylon and Daniel
was one of those prisoners.

The king ordered his chief official to select from
among the Israelite exiles some young men of the
royal family and of the noble families. They had to
be handsome, intelligent, well-trained, quick to
learn, and free from physical defects, so that they
would be qualified to serve in the royal court.

Daniel was one of those chosen.

The king also gave orders that every day they were to be given the same food and wine as the members of the royal court. After three years of this training they were to appear before the king.

Daniel 1:8 says that Daniel made up his mind not to let himself become ritually unclean by eating food and wine as the members of the royal court, so he asked the king's chief official to help him.

God made the official sympathetic to Daniel. However he was afraid of the king, so he said to Daniel, 'The king has decided what you are to eat and drink, and if you don't look as fit as the other young men, he may kill me.'

So Daniel went to the guard whom the chief official had placed in charge of him and his three friends. 'Test us for ten days.' When the time was up, they looked healthier and stronger than all those who had been eating the royal food. So from then on the guard let them continue to eat vegetables instead of what the king provided.

What really mattered to Daniel was God's smile. That was the top priority and the guiding principle of his life and behaviour. He had decided that nothing which would displease the Lord would have any place in his life. So he made up his mind to please the Lord in any situation no matter the cost or consequence.

Some things are not negotiable

There would be nothing wrong with the king's food. In fact it was probably the best that money could buy. However it had probably been dedicated to an idol.

The prayer said before it was eaten would probably have taken the form of saying thank you to a false god; and Daniel would have thought that this would be denying that his God was God!

Because he believed that the most important thing in life is to please God, he made up his mind, no matter the cost or outcome, not to eat and drink. To other people he may have appeared narrow minded. Why couldn't he just eat the food and believe God inwardly? Why be so fussy about a plate of food?

Daniel lived by faith and not by sight. Which meant that he saw beyond the food and recognised that in every situation his actions and decisions would either express loyalty or disloyalty to his LORD.

Loyalty was non-negotiable. He had made up his mind to please God. He had remembered his Creator while he was still young and had seized the day.

He prayed to God

This is another part of his life that has impressed and influenced me.

He was a teenager when his land and his people were invaded. And because Nebuchadnezzar had adopted this policy of enlisting the most promising young men of his new empire for his government, whatever their nationality, Daniel found himself away from home, separated from family, a hostage and an exile in a strange land.

In that horrible and difficult situation, he made up his mind to please and pray to God.

In fact prayer seems to be his normal reaction to every situation.

The King's dream

King Nebuchadnezzar had a dream that worried him so much that he couldn't sleep, so he sent for his fortune-tellers, magicians, sorcerers and wizards to come and explain the dream to him. He wanted his advisers to tell him both what the dream had been and what its meaning was! He then added, 'If you can't, I'll have you torn limb from limb and make your houses a pile of ruins. But if you can tell me both the dream and its meaning, I will reward you with gifts and great honour.'

The advisers replied that no one on the face of the earth could tell the king what he wanted to know. At that, the king flew into a rage and ordered the execution of all the royal advisers in Babylon, which included Daniel and his friends.

Daniel went at once and obtained royal permission for more time, so that he could tell the king what the dream meant.

Then he went home and told his friends Hananiah, Mishael and Azariah what had happened. He told them to pray to the God of heaven for mercy and to ask him to explain the mystery to them so that they would not be killed along with the other advisers in Babylon. That same night the mystery was revealed to Daniel in a vision!

God answered his prayer and showed him what to tell the king. Daniel was so excited by what God had done that he praised the God of heaven with these words:

'God is wise and powerful!
    praise him for ever and ever.
He controls the times and seasons;
    he makes and unmakes kings;
    it is he who gives wisdom and understanding.
He reveals things that are deep and secret;
    he knows what is hidden in darkness,
    and he himself is surrounded by light.
I praise you, and honour you, God of my
ancestors.
You have given me wisdom and strength;
    you have answered my prayer
    and shown us what to tell the king.'
(Daniel 2: 20-23 G.N.B.)

110

So he went to Arioch, whom the king had commanded to execute the royal advisers and said to him, 'Don't put them to death. Take me to the king, and I will tell him what his dream means.'

Arioch took Daniel, at once, into King Nebuchadnezzar's presence, introduced him and Daniel was allowed to speak.

Imagine the scene! Daniel, in his late teens, an exile in a strange land, a hostage, a prisoner, separated from his mum and dad and standing in front of someone like Saddam Hussein! How would we have felt? How did he feel?

Daniel seized the day and said with great courage, boldness and faith, 'Your Majesty, there is no wizard, magician, fortune-teller or astrologer who can tell you what you dreamt and what it means. But there is a God in heaven who reveals mysteries. He has informed Your Majesty what will happen in the future. Now I will tell you the dream, the vision you had while you were asleep.

'In your vision you saw standing before you a giant statue, bright and shining, and terrifying to look at. His head was made of the finest gold; its chest and arms were made of silver; its waist and hips of bronze; its legs of iron, and its feet partly of iron and partly of clay.

'While you were looking at it, a great stone broke loose from a cliff without anyone touching it, struck the iron and clay feet of the statue and shattered them. At once the iron, clay, bronze, silver and gold crumbled and became like dust on a threshing place in summer. The wind carried it all away, leaving not a trace. But the stone grew to be a mountain that covered the whole earth.

'This was the dream. Now I will tell Your Majesty what it means.

'You are the greatest of all kings. The God of heaven has made you emperor and given you power, might and honour. He has made you ruler of all the inhabited earth and ruler over all the animals and birds. You are the head of gold.'

He then proceeded to reveal that there would be a second, a third and a fourth empire, all symbolised as different metals and different parts of the giant statue.

Finally, with amazing authority he said, '... the God of heaven will establish a kingdom that will never end. It will never be conquered, but will completely destroy all those empires, and then last for ever ... The Great God is telling Your Majesty what will happen in the future.

'I have told you exactly what you dreamt, and have given you its meaning.'

Not bad for a teenager, separated from his family in an alien culture, imprisoned by the super-power of his day and standing before the most powerful man in the world.

King Nebuchadnezzar bowed to the ground

and said, 'Your God is the greatest of all gods, the Lord over kings, and the one who reveals mysteries. I know this because you have been able to explain this mystery.'

Then he gave Daniel a high position, presented him with lots of fabulous gifts, put him in charge of the province of Babylon, made him the head of all the royal advisers at the royal court.

Not bad for a teenager who had made up his mind to please God no matter what.

A person in process, under pressure and moving towards maturity and his God-given potential. All because he seized the day.

Dead Poets Society

In this film, Robin Williams, who appeared in *Awakenings* and *Good Morning Vietnam*; plays the role of the new English teacher at Welton Preparatory School in the USA.

John Keating sets about teaching his class with unusual techniques, style and enthusiasm.

On the first lesson, he takes the class of boys down to the photograph and trophy room. As they watch and listen to his inspiring and humorous lesson, he has them look at a poem and in particular one verse.

He then selects one line from the poem which reads, 'Gather ye rosebuds while ye may.'

'Boys,' he continues, 'look at the men in the

photographs, dead and gone; and recognise that we also are food for worms.

'You are young. Full of hormones. Full of ideas. One day, however, you also will be fertilising daffodils.

'Listen to them as they whisper their legacy, *Carpe diem*, "Seize the day".'

Remember your Creator while you are still young. Recognise your potential. Look at and learn from Daniel and seize the day!

Prayer

Dear Father,
I want to remember you as my Creator while I am still young. Help me to do so more and more and day by day.

Thank you for Daniel's example and challenge. Help me to seize the day in terms of obeying, pleasing and serving you.
Carpe diem.
Amen.

Questions

1. Name an area or areas in you life where you need to 'make up your mind' to please God rather than yourself or others.

2. Describe your attitude to prayer.

3. Highlight three answers to prayer in the last three months.

4. How about you praying three times a day like Daniel? Read Daniel 6 and ask God to speak to you about your prayer life. (Go on, it will only take 8 minutes.)

Living

on

God's   Video

Chapter   10

Introducing a king and queen

It was the third year of his reign and he decided to give a banquet for all his officials, administrators, army personnel and the governors and noblemen of his 127 provinces.

There were loads of people and, believe it or not, his banquet lasted six months. His provinces stretched all the way from India to Sudan and they came in their hundreds to celebrate and experience the wealth, splendour and majesty of the imperial court.

After that, the king gave a banquet for all the men, rich and poor alike, in his capital city. It lasted a whole week and was held in the gardens of the royal palace.

The Bible tells us that the courtyard was decorated with blue and white cotton curtains, paved with marble and had couches made of gold and silver placed in it. Drinks were served in gold cups which were designed in such a way that no two of them were alike. The king was extremely generous with the drinks and ordered the palace servants to give everyone as much as he wanted.

Meanwhile, inside the royal palace Queen Vashti was giving a banquet for the women. If the banquet for the men was as I've described, you can imagine what it would have been like for the women.

On the seventh day of his banquet, the king had gone a bit too far with the alcohol and was feeling rather merry. So he called in the seven eunuchs, who were his personal servants, and ordered them to bring in Queen Vashti, wearing her royal crown. He did this we are told, because she was a beautiful woman and he wanted to show off her beauty to the officials and all his guests.

When the servants told the queen of the king's command, she refused to come. The king was furious and, as it was his custom to ask for expert advice on questions of law and order, he called in his advisors. He said to these men, 'I, King Xerxes, sent my servants to Queen Vashti with a command, and she refused to obey it! What does the law say that we should do with her?'

His seven advisors who were from Persia and Media, held the highest positions in the kingdom. Their counsel was that the queen had insulted the king, his officials and every man in the empire; that soon every woman in the empire would begin to look down on her husband as soon as she heard what the queen had done. They then encouraged the king to issue a royal proclamation, written into the laws of Persia and Media so that it could never be changed, that Vashti should never again appear before the king. They concluded by saying that Queen Vashti should be replaced by a better woman.

As a result of this advice a message was sent, by the king, to each of the royal provinces saying that every husband should be the master of his home and speak with final authority.

After the king's anger had cooled down, he kept thinking about what Vashti had done and about his proclamation against her. In the process of this, some of his advisors suggested, 'Why don't you make a search to find some beautiful young virgins? Then take the girl you like best and make her queen in Vashti's place.'

The king thought this was good advice, so he followed it.

Enter Esther

Officials were appointed in every province of the empire and ordered to bring all these beautiful young girls to the king's harem in Susa, the capital city.

Living in Susa was a Jew named Mordecai. He had been captured and exiled when King Nebuchadnezzar of Babylon had taken King Jehoiachin of Judah into exile from Jerusalem.

Esther was his cousin, and at the death of her parents, Mordecai had adopted her and brought her up as his own daughter.

She was a cracker! The Bible says that she was a beautiful girl and had a good figure. Along with other girls, she was put in the royal palace.

Hegai, who was in charge of the harem, liked Esther, and she won his favour. As a result, he gave her the best place in the harem, assigned seven girls to serve her and began, immediately, her beauty treatment of massage and special diet.

The regular beauty treatment for the girls lasted a year. After that, each one would be taken in turn to the king. When she went from the harem to the palace, she could wear whatever she wanted. She would go in the evening, and the next morning would be taken to another harem where the king's concubines were housed. She would not go to the king again unless he liked her enough to ask for her by name.

Can you imagine that? One year of preparation for one night in bed with a tyrant king whose reputation for weird sexual activity was common knowledge.

The moment came for young Esther to go to the king. It was the tenth month during Xerxes' seventh year that she was brought to the royal palace. She wore exactly what Hegai the eunuch in charge advised her to wear.

I wonder how she felt? What would her mind have been thinking?

Whatever she was thinking and however she felt, the king liked her more than anyone else. In fact, more than any of the others, she won his favour and affection.

As a result, he placed the royal crown on her head and made her queen in place of Vashti. He gave a great banquet in her honour, invited all his officials, proclaimed a holiday, gave gifts to the poor and made a tax cut.

Enter Haman

About five years go by and the king appoints a man named Haman to the position of Prime Minister. The nation he belonged to were traditional enemies of the Jews. For some reason the king ordered all the officials in his service to show their respect for Haman by kneeling and bowing to him. Everyone did except Mordecai the Jew.

Haman hated the Jews and as a result of Mordecai's behaviour towards him he began to concentrate his hatred on Mordecai, who was by

121

now one of the king's administrators. His hatred grew to such a size and intensity that he made plans to kill every Jew in the whole Persian empire.

The king, who was known for his crazy ideas and his unpredictable and violent temper, agreed to Haman's plans. On a single day, the thirteenth of Adar, all Jews, young and old, women and children were to be killed. They were to be slaughtered without mercy and their belongings were to be taken.

When Mordecai heard of it, he tore his clothes (a sign of great distress and sadness). He then dressed in sackcloth (a sign of prayer and repentance), covered his head with ashes and went through the city wailing loudly and bitterly.

Esther's servant girls told her what he was doing and she was deeply disturbed. She sent one of the palace eunuchs to find out what was happening and why. Mordecai told him everything and also how much money Haman had promised to put into the royal treasury if all the Jews were killed. He told him to ask Esther to go and plead with the king and beg him to have mercy on her people.

Mordecai was asking Esther to do a very dangerous thing. For if anyone went to the inner courtyard of the royal palace and saw the king without being summoned, that person had to die. That was the law.

There was only one way to get round the law. If the king held out his gold sceptre to the person, then, their life was spared.

Esther was aware that it had been a month since the king had sent for her, so she sent a message to Mordecai reminding him of the law and informing him of how long it had been since she had seen the king.

When he received her message he replied with a warning which went something like this. 'Don't imagine that you are safer than any other Jew just because you are in the royal palace. If you keep quiet at a time like this, help will come from heaven to the Jews, and they will be saved, but you will die and your father's family will come to an end. Yet who knows, maybe it was for a time like this that you were made queen.'

Esther's response was to ask Mordecai to gather all the Jews to Susa together to hold a fast and pray for three days and nights. She promised that she and her servant-girls would do the same and afterwards she would go to the king, even though it was against the law. She then said something very courageous, 'If I must die for doing it I will die.'

On the third day of her fast she put on her royal robes and went and stood in the inner courtyard of the palace, facing the throne room.

The king was inside, on his royal throne, facing the entrance. When he saw Queen Esther standing outside, she won his favour, and he held out to her the golden sceptre. She then moved in and touched the tip of it.

Esther's Banquets

He asked her what she wanted and she replied with an invite to a banquet for two. She simply wanted the king and Haman to be her guests that night, at a banquet she was preparing for them.

The king ordered Haman to attend.

While they were drinking wine, the king asked her again what she wanted. He offered to give her anything she wanted, even if it was to have half his empire!

She replied with another invite to a banquet for two. The same two, the same place, the next night; promising to tell him then what she wanted.

Remarkable things were to take place during the night between the two banquets.

Haman left the first banquet happy and in a good mood. As he was leaving the palace he saw Mordecai who refused to rise and show any sign of respect for him. This made him furious.

On arriving home, he invited his friends to his house and boasted about his wealth, family, promotion to high office and his private banquets with the king and the queen. Then he added, 'But none of this means a thing to me as long as I see that Jew, Mordecai, sitting at the entrance of the palace.'

On hearing this, his wife and friends suggested that he built a massive gallows and asked the king to have Mordecai hanged on it. He thought this was a good idea and went ahead with it.

That same night the king could not get to sleep, so he ordered the official records of the empire to be brought and read to him.

The part they read included the account of how Mordecai had uncovered a plot to assassinate the king approximately two years previous to this.

The king asked, 'How have we honoured and rewarded Mordecai for this?'

His servants answered, 'Nothing has been done for him.'

'Are any of my officials in the palace?' the king asked.

Haman had just entered the courtyard. He had come to ask the king to have Mordecai hanged. So the servants told him that Haman was there and was waiting to see the king.

'Show him in,' the king said.

What happened from here on in is simply remarkable.

The king asked Haman what should be done for someone whom the king wants to honour.

Haman thinks it's him. 'Why, this person should be put on the king's horse, robed in the king's robes, wear a crown on his head and be led by the king's highest nobleman through the city square announcing that this man is honoured by the king.'

The king then orders Haman to do exactly this for Mordecai the Jew.

Later that evening, Haman then had to attend Esther's second banquet. During the banquet she at last tells the king about the plot to destroy her people and reveals that it's Haman.

The king is furious. Haman is terrified. He throws himself on the queen's couch to beg for mercy while the king walks in rage through the palace gardens wondering what to do.

King Xerxes returns, thinks that Haman is trying to rape Esther and orders his execution.

One of the king's eunuchs tells his majesty of the gallows that Haman built for Mordecai.

'Hang Haman on it,' the king commanded.

So Haman was hanged on the gallows he had built for Mordecai.

King Xerxes gave Queen Esther all Haman's property. On hearing that Mordecai and Esther were related, he took off his ring with his seal and gave it to Mordecai and allowed him entry into his presence. A new decree was written that rescued the Jews from destruction and took effect on the day that was set for their slaughter.

Living on God's Video
Now that you know most of the story of Esther, you may be asking why on earth I've called this

chapter 'Living on God's Video'. The reason is because of the word *providence*.

Probably the outstanding feature of this book in the Bible is the fact that there is not one single reference to God! God is never mentioned.

However, just because he isn't referred to does not mean that he isn't present and active. He may not be in the words and syllables, but he is in the story. The word to describe this kind of activity that God is engaged in is *providence*.

It comes from the Latin *provideo*: *video* - I see, *pro* - on behalf of or before.

God's providential activity means that God is seeing to it in advance that all things will work together for the good because Esther loves God. He is working providentially on her and her people's behalf. You can see this in a variety of ways.

* What happens when she loses her mum and dad?
* What happens when she ends up in the king's harem?
* What happens when she goes before the king without being called?
* What happens when Haman plots to kill Mordecai?
* What happens when the king can't sleep?

Esther means 'a star'. And as she seeks to follow

and be faithful to her God, in a painful, tough, mysterious and dangerous situation, she becomes his star in his video!

As a young woman, she doesn't see herself as a pawn or a victim; but as a person in process and definitely under pressure. As she trusts that God is, even when it looks like he isn't, she begins to discover her God-given potential.

Right now you are living on God's video and he wants you to shine as his star wherever you are and whatever your situation.

Prayer

Dear Father,
Thank you for your providential activity in my life. It's good to know that you not only see, but you will see to it in advance that all things will work together for good because I love you.

Help me to shine no matter what!
For the honour of Jesus, I pray.
Amen!

Question

1) How many times in this chapter did Esther win favour with someone? (You may want to underline them as you find them.)

2) How can this be true in your life?

Little
is
Large

Chapter 11

It was a Sunday evening and we had travelled about six miles to a neighbouring town to attend a special meeting.

The man who was preaching that night was an elderly Scottish evangelist. He was gentle and spoke softly and sincerely.

I was a teenager and I remember that I sat near the back on the left. I wasn't too excited about being there and had already made up my mind that this old boy would be a bit boring.

However, this was to be a message and a man that I would never forget.

His major theme was about God using young people and little things - he began to show the potential of both, when God uses them.

I was young and felt quite insignificant in the big wide world. As he spoke I began to see that God could use me and the little things that I could do in serving him and his world.

A little boy who gave what he had

The old preacher talked about the day Jesus went across Lake Galilee, climbed a hill and sat down with his disciples. A large crowd followed him and he turned to his disciples and asked them where they could buy enough food to feed all the people.

Andrew told the Lord Jesus that there was a boy who had five loaves of barley bread and two fishes.

Jesus got the people to sit down on the grass. He then took the bread, gave thanks to God, and distributed it to the people who were sitting there. He did the same with the fish, and they all had as much as they wanted.

You probably know the rest of the story. At least five thousand men were fed. There could easily have been another five thousand women and children. When they were all full, the disciples filled twelve baskets with the pieces over.

I can still hear the preacher say, as if I was the only person in the audience, 'You can be like that little boy by giving all that you are and have and ever hope to be to Jesus'.

A little girl who told what she knew

Naaman, the commander of the Syrian army, was highly respected by the king of Syria, because through Naaman the Lord had given victory to the Syrian forces. He was a great soldier, but he suffered from a dreaded skin disease.

In one of their raids against Israel, the Syrians had carried off a little Israelite girl, who became a servant of Naaman's wife.

One day she said to her mistress, 'I wish that my master could go to the prophet who lives in Samaria. He would cure him of his disease.'

As a result of this little girl, Naaman went to see the prophet, Elisha.

With his horses and chariot, he stopped at the entrance to Elisha's house. Elisha sent a servant out to tell him to go and wash himself seven times in the River Jordan, and he would be completely cured of his disease.

The big army commander was rather angry, to say the least, that the prophet himself did not come out and that the Jordan river was filthy.

Eventually, he went down to the Jordan, dipped himself in it seven times as instructed, and was completely cured.

Centuries later, when Jesus was on earth, he provided some incredible information about this unnamed little girl in 2 Kings 5 in the Old Testament. This is what he said: 'And there were many people suffering from a dreaded skin disease who lived in Israel during the time of the prophet Elisha; yet not one of them was healed, but only Naaman the Syrian' (Luke 4:27 G.N.B.).

Imagine that! Nobody before or after Naaman was cured of this dreaded skin disease except him. How did that little girl know? Why did she bother to help the people who had stolen her from her mum and dad and removed her from her own town, people and country?

I'm not sure about the answers to those questions except to say that she simply told what she knew. It's the only thing that God has allowed us to know that she did.

It seemed such a small thing, yet had huge consequences.

The old Scottish evangelist looked down from the stage in the Town Hall, as if there was only me to look at and said, 'If you will simply tell what you know about the Lord, other people in your generation will be changed as Naaman was and come to know God for themselves. There is great potential in young people and little things when God uses them.'

Terry Waite and the postcard

It was so moving to see him arrive at RAF Lyneham in November 1991, after 1,763 days in chains. As I watched and listened to his speech, I remembered what a friend of mine told me a number of years ago: 'Little is much if God is in it'.

Terry Waite told how he was kept in total and complete isolation for four years. He saw and spoke to no-one apart from the odd word with his guards.

Then one day out of the blue, a guard came with a postcard. It showed a stained glass window from Bedford showing John Bunyan in jail.

There was a message on it from someone he didn't know, simply saying, 'We remember, we shall not forget. We shall continue to pray for you and to work for all people who are detained around the world'.

He then added, 'I can tell you, that thought, that sent me back to the marvellous work of agencies like Amnesty International and their letter-writing campaigns and I would say never despise those simple actions. Something, somewhere will get through to the people you are concerned about.'

'Never despise those simple actions' because 'Little is much if God is in it.'

Small enough for God to use

For centuries, God has been doing big things with small things and young people. This is his way in history.

For example:

* When God wanted to deliver his people from Egypt, (two million of them), he sent in a baby not an army. Baby Moses was God's big plan (see Exodus, chapters 1-3).

* Disobedience was bringing disaster to God's people, especially through the sinful lives of the spiritual leaders. God's answer in that situation was to send in a boy called Samuel.

1 Samuel 3: 19-21 says:

'As Samuel grew up, the Lord was with him and made everything that Samuel said come true. So all the people of Israel, from one end of the country to the other, knew that Samuel was indeed a prophet of the Lord. The Lord continued to reveal himself at Shiloh, where he had appeared to Samuel and had spoken to him. And when Samuel spoke, all Israel listened' (G.N.B.).

* A giant soldier was bringing terror to God's army. An entire army was paralysed with fear. Nobody would take up the challenge he gave of engaging in one-to-one conflict with him.

Along comes a shepherd boy called David and accepts the challenge to fight him.

1 Samuel 17:42 says that when Goliath 'got a good look at David, he was filled with scorn for him because he was just a nice, good-looking boy'.

That day, that shepherd boy stood in front of that three meter tall soldier and said:

'You are coming against me with sword, spear and javelin, but I come against you in the name of the Lord Almighty, the God of the Israelite armies, which you have defied. This very day the Lord will put you in my power; I will defeat you and cut off your head. And I will give the bodies of the Philistine soldiers to the birds and animals to eat. Then the whole world will know that Israel has a God, and everyone here will see that the Lord does not need swords or spears to save his people. He is victorious in battle, and he will put all of you in our power' (1 Samuel 17:45-47 G.N.B.).

I'm sure you know what took place next. But let me remind you what verse 50 says: 'And so, without a sword, David defeated and killed Goliath with a catapult and a stone!'

God's foolishness and weakness

In the fast moving, media-saturated, image-conscious, noise-dependent, lonely-peopled, man-centred, solo-living, possessions-dominated, three-minute-cultured and power-orientated western world, God's style and strategy is often unwanted and mostly forgotten.

But God's timeless truth is superbly summed up in the words of the apostle Paul, when he wrote to the church in Corinth. (Corinth was a great cosmopolitan Greek city, the capital of the Roman province of Achaia. It was noted for its thriving commerce, proud culture, widespread immorality and multi-faith society.)

'For what seems to be God's foolishness is wiser than human wisdom, and what seems to be God's weakness is stronger than human strength.

Now remember what you were, my brothers, when God called you. From the human point of view few of you were wise or powerful or of high social standing.

God purposely chose what the world considers nonsense in order to shame the wise, and he chose what the world considers weak in order to shame the powerful. He chose what the world looks down on and despised and thinks is nothing, in order to destroy what the world thinks is important.

This means that no-one can boast in God's presence... Whoever wants to boast must boast of what the Lord has done' (1 Cor 1:25-31 G.N.B.).

What ultimately matters therefore, is neither my inability nor ability, but my attitude and avail-ability to God!

Prayer

Heavenly Father,

Thank you for your unique style and strategy for my life. Thank you for demonstrating it so clearly in Jesus!

I want to be small enough and available for you to use. Teach me your ways. Show me your paths. Guide me in your truth.

Make me usable and through me bring your love, peace, justice and forgiveness to the world.

Amen!

Question

(1) According to Matthew 10:42 what did Jesus say will certainly receive a reward?

(2) What do you think this means for us today?

Keep
Doing
the Basics

Chapter 12

Brian Clough is a famous, very skilled and at times, controversial English football manager. A number of years ago, during a TV interview, he was asked to explain, what he would do, if he was invited to manage a football team that wasn't scoring goals and winning matches.

He replied that he would first of all go over and check out whether each player knew and was doing the basics.

"Basics, like training habits, ball skills, knowing their position in the team, understanding the basic team rules and moves, playing to the plan and obeying the boss. I would teach what needed to be taught, change what needed to be changed, encourage those needing encouragement and be with and help them with all I can give.

"Basically, I would make sure they are doing the basics extremely well, then I would tell them to keep doing the basics! If they do that, sooner or later, they will start scoring goals and winning matches."

That's like following Jesus!

We have been discovering that young people are people in process, people under pressure and people with potential.

If we are to maintain progress in the process, cope well with the pressures and discover our God-given potential, we will have to keep doing the basics in following Jesus.

That's what Timothy did as he went through the process, struggled with the pressures and discovered his God-given potential.

Timothy: the jig-saw pieces

These are the jig-saw pieces of information the New Testament provides, which make up the picture of his life.

* He was the child of a mixed marriage. His mum was a Jewess and his dad was a Greek (Acts 16:1).

* He had never been circumcised as a Jewish child (Acts 16:3). That could indicate some of the differences and tensions between his mum and dad.

* His mum and grandmother really loved and trusted God (2 Tim 1:5).

* His home was in Lystra (Acts 16:1). We don't know for definite how he became a follower of Christ. We do know that the apostle Paul visited Lystra on his first missionary journey. Perhaps it was through him that Timothy started to worship the Lord Jesus! (2 Tim 3:10-11). Perhaps this is why Paul refers to him as 'my true son in the faith' (1 Tim 1:2).

* Paul chose him as one of his assistants and travelling companions (1 Tim 4:14; 2 Tim 1:6; Acts 16:3).

* He was sent on special missions to strengthen and encourage churches (1 Thess 3:2; 1 Cor 16:10-11).

* Like everybody else, he had his problems!

We know that Timothy as a young man, was in process, under pressure and discovering his potential like the rest of us. In his period of 'growth to maturity' he had to handle a few delicate issues.

Handling his hormones

Obviously he had to face the temptations that all young people face.

It is possible, however, that he tended to hang about a bit too long when he was being tempted. Perhaps, because of his sheltered upbringing, he was naive to the dangers that temptation presented. It could be that he really struggled with self-control.

Why else would Paul say to him, 'Flee the evil desires of youth' (2 Tim 2:22 N.I.V.).

Handling his health

He was definitely not your Frank Bruno-type of person. He was probably the exact opposite.

It seems that he was far from being strong and healthy. In one of his letters to him, Paul had to write, 'Do not drink water only, but take a little wine to help your digestion, since you are so often ill' (1 Tim 5:23 G.N.B.).

Handling his shyness

As a companion for his youthful lusts and poor health, and perhaps as a consequence of them, was shyness and timidity.

There were times, it seems, as he served the Lord, that this part of his make-up almost paralysed his service. As a result, Paul said to the Corinthian church,

'If Timothy comes, see to it that he has nothing to fear while he is with you, for he is carrying on the work of the Lord as I am. No one should refuse to accept him. Send him on his way in peace so that he may return to me' (1 Cor 16:10-11 N.I.V.).

In a personal letter to him, he had to be reminded that 'God did not give us a spirit of timidity, but a spirit of power, of love, and of self-discipline' (2 Tim 1:7 N.I.V.).

Imagine that kind of thing happening today. A world-famous evangelist sends one of his associates to a church that has lots of problems, in order to set up a crusade.

He writes in his introductory letter, 'You will discover that my associate has a number of difficulties in relating and getting to know other people. He is shy and timid, has poor health and has to strictly avoid situations of temptation. If he is to work successfully with you, please give him an extra-special welcome, don't look down on him because he is young, make it easy for him as he works through his shyness and timidity.'

Timothy doesn't appear to be the trendy, multi-gifted, good looking and charismatic personality that we might expect and want him to be. He seems to be so unlike what an ideal Christian and servant of Christ ought to be in 20th Century terms.

With these sorts of personal problems to face, it's amazing that he kept on going. But like Brian Clough, the apostle Paul kept encouraging Timothy to 'keep doing the basics'.

What were those basics? Well, I've picked out some from the two letters that he wrote to this young 'man of God'. They read something like this.

Keep yourself in training for a godly life (1 Tim 4:7).
Godliness is recognising and having respect for who God is and living conscious of who he is. It's taking God seriously so that your respect for him

functions in every room and through every day of your life.

Obviously it does not come automatically or Paul would never have told Timothy to keep himself in training. It involves digging into God's Word. Check out Psalm 119 to find a godly person's view of God's Word. It means finding out more about God's world.

Nearly two years ago while we were having our tea, a bird started singing in our back garden. We opened the back door to discover a blackbird sitting on the roof of a neighbour's house. It was beautiful!

Timothy, my little boy, not the one in the Bible, asked if it was singing for us! I jumped up from the table to get a book on birds. There I found the following information.

The best song months for a blackbird stretch from late February to early July. Its song is a rich, sweet succession of whistling phrases with piping notes. It is usually sung from a tree or a building. It often leads the dawn or evening chorus.

That evening, as I was putting Timothy to bed, we did our normal evening prayers. As we began to work our way through the day, thanking God for the things we thought were appropriate, he said, "Dear Jesus, thank you for Mr Blackbird!" And I suddenly realised, that is the beginning of godliness.

Take your part in suffering, as a loyal soldier of Christ Jesus (2 Tim 2:3).

I don't exactly know if his timidity and shyness made him hold back from spreading the Good News about Jesus, but it seems that it may have. 2 Timothy 1:8 reads, 'Do not be ashamed, then, of witnessing for our Lord; nor be ashamed of me, a prisoner for Christ's sake. Instead, take your part in suffering for the Good News, as God gives you the strength to do it' (G.N.B.).

Paul's prison experiences had given him a big opportunity to watch Roman soldiers and think about the parallel between the soldier and the follower of Jesus.

In earlier letters that he wrote, he refers to the Christian soldier's battle with principalities and powers, the armour to wear as well as the weapons to use. (Eph 6:11ff; 1 Tim 1:18; 2 Cor 6:7; 10: 3-5).

But to Timothy, he says, 'Take your part in suffering, as a loyal soldier of Christ Jesus. A soldier on active service wants to please his commanding officer and so does not get mixed up in the affairs of civilian life' (2 Tim 2:3-4 G.N.B.).

Soldiers on active service do not expect a safe or easy time. They take risk, hardship, and suffering as the normal experience of a soldier.

It was Tertullian who once said, 'No soldier comes to the war surrounded by luxuries, nor goes into action from a comfortable bedroom, but from the makeshift and narrow tent, where every kind of hardness and severity and unpleasantness is to be found.'

As followers of Jesus, we should not expect an easy time.

In 1982 the Falklands war took place. It was a time of national crisis for us in Great Britain. After it was all over, ITV presented a 'Tuesday Special' documentary entitled *The Untold Story*. During that programme, one of the soldiers from the paras told an untold part of the battle.

The marines and paras had to 'yomp' from San Carlos Bay across the rugged terrain of East Falkland to Port Stanley. The Argentinian Army had built a ring of defences round Port Stanley at Tumbledown Mountain, Wireless Ridge and Mount Longdon. After hard fighting against well dug-in defenders, the British soldiers saw large numbers of the enemy streaming back to Stanley and soon white flags began to appear. Victory had been achieved.

'Yomping' is the term they use for marching, with heavy packs on their backs. They had to 'yomp' at least thirty miles across the island.

In doing that, a major problem was drinking water. The sterilising tablets they were using were not working and as a result, most of them had diarrhoea.

To cope with this, they cut their trousers at the

crutch and kept on going. As they marched, heading for battle, they drank and ate at one end of their bodies and it poured out at the other end.

At this point, the soldier telling the story broke down and wept, and asked for the cameras to be cut.

Suffering and soldiering go together - it's normal and to be expected. The disciple of Jesus should not expect an easy time if he or she is going to be loyal to the Lord!

Elderly friends of mine in Scotland have often talked about what they experienced as children during the Second World War. There was no extravagance. They had to be careful with money, food, clothes, sweets and entertainment. Because of the crisis and emergency, self-denial was normal and expected.

Frequently, when they asked for more food or demanded sweets they were told 'there's a war on'! That was the phrase that shaped their world view and expectations, values, relationships and priorities.

Because 'there's a war on', young Timothy is told not to 'get mixed up in the affairs of civilian life'. That does not mean he should dodge his ordinary duties at home, in school, at work or in the community or forfeit good wholesome pleasures.

What is being forbidden, for the loyal soldier of Jesus, are things that hinder him or her from fighting Christ's battles. Things, relationships, practices, activities that cool our love for Christ and spoil our service for him can so easily hold us back. Feeding the hungry, clothing the naked, helping the poor and homeless, spreading the Good News and bringing justice into God's world can so easily slide down or slip off our agenda if we become disloyal to Jesus.

Perhaps this is why Paul says to this young follower of Jesus, 'Remember Jesus Christ...' (2 Tim 2:8).

Because Jesus said 'no' to what he wanted and 'yes' to what his Father wanted, his suffering has brought joy and his death has brought life to us.

"So, Timothy," the old apostle seems to be saying, "when you are tempted to dodge pain, obedience, humiliation, suffering or sacrifice as a loyal soldier, remember Jesus Christ and think twice!"

So what's next?

It's been my privilege and pleasure to have spent time with you through this book. I hope it has helped and encouraged you to keep on going.

So what's next for you in the process you are in, the pressures you face and the potential you are discovering? Whatever it is, 'keep doing the basics'! I've only mentioned two, check out 2 Timothy for some more.

If you 'keep doing the basics' sooner or later you will score goals and win matches. You won't simply grow old, you will grow up to be like Christ in character and conduct.

Keep on going!

Prayer

Father,

Thank you for teaching me about the process I'm in, some of the pressures I experience and the potential you have planted in me.

Show me what's next for me and help me to keep doing the basics. Teach me other basics.

Make me like Christ in character and conduct I pray. Give me wisdom and strength to be loyal to Jesus.

Amen.

Questions

(1) What 'basics' have you established in your life?

(2) How and by when can you improve in this area of your life?

(3) Complete the statements: As a result of reading this book:

(a) I have learned _____

(b) I will change/do _____